KETO FAT BOMBS

Ketogenic Diet Fat Bombs That You Must Prepare Before Any Other!

(Desserts, Snacks and Recipes for High Fat Low Carb Diet)

James Craig

Published by Sharon Lohan

© James Craig

All Rights Reserved

Keto Fat Bombs: Ketogenic Diet Fat Bombs That You Must Prepare Before Any Other! (Desserts, Snacks and Recipes for High Fat Low Carb Diet)

ISBN 978-1-990334-18-4

All rights reserved. No part of this guide may be reproduced in any form without permission in writing from the publisher except in the case of brief quotations embodied in critical articles or reviews.

Legal & Disclaimer

The information contained in this book is not designed to replace or take the place of any form of medicine or professional medical advice. The information in this book has been provided for educational and entertainment purposes only.

The information contained in this book has been compiled from sources deemed reliable, and it is accurate to the best of the Author's knowledge; however, the Author cannot guarantee its accuracy and validity and cannot be held liable for any errors or omissions. Changes are periodically made to this book. You must consult your doctor or get professional medical advice before using any of the suggested remedies, techniques, or information in this book.

Table of contents

Part 1 1
Introduction 2
Eating keto food you will see more benefits, such as: 5
About the keto fat bombs 9
Meat keto fat bombs 13
Lamb and Cheese Fat Bombs 13
Calories: 189 14
Smoked Sausages Fat Bombs 15
Spicy Bacon Fat Bombs 17
Chicken Breast Fat Bombs 19
Smoked Bacon and Peanuts Fat Bombs 21
Smoked Ham Fat Bombs 23
Bacon and Turkey Breast Fat Bombs 25
Beef Meat Keto Fat Bombs 27
Bacon and Pecan Nuts Fat Bombs 29
Calories: 162 30
Chicken Livers Fat Bombs 30
Bacon and Walnuts Fat Bombs 33
Calories: 175 34
Dried Plums and Bacon Fat Bombs 35
Bacon and Parmesan Cheese Fat Bombs 37
Grilled Fat Bombs 39
Salami Fat Bombs 41
Calories: 159 42
Fish and seafood keto fat bombs 43

Mackerel Fat Bombs 43

Mackerel and Lemon Fat Bombs 45

Sardines Fat Bombs 47

Sea Perch Fat Bombs 49

Crab Meat Fat Bombs 50

Salmon and Cucumber Fat Bombs 52

Tuna and Salmon Fat Bombs 54

Pacific Halibut Fat Bombs 56

Crème Fat Bombs 57

Herrings Fat Bombs 59

Tuna and Caviar Fat Bombs 61

Calories: 133 62

Tuna and Zucchini Fat Bombs 62

Calories: 149 63

Spicy Shrimps Fat Bombs 64

Mackerel and Eggs Fat Bombs 66

Shrimps Fat Bombs 68

Vegetable keto fat bombs 70

Cucumber and Tomato Fat Bombs 70

Spicy Peanuts Fat Bombs 72

Garlic and Cheese Fat Bombs 74

Calories: 98 75

Sunflower Seeds Fat Bombs 76

Fried Brie Cheese Fat Bombs 78

Tomatoes Fat Bombs 80

Calories: 115 81

Pumpkin Seeds Fat Bombs 82

Calories: 147 ... 83
Dried Tomatoes Fat Bombs ... 84
Calories: 123 ... 85
Pumpkin Fat Bombs ... 85
Spicy Chili and Coconut Fat Bombs ... 87
Conclusion ... 89
Part 2 ... 90
Introduction ... 91
Chapter 1: what is a keto fat bomb? ... 92
Chapter 2: sweet keto fat bomb recipes ... 95
Almond Joy Fat Bombs (Serves 12) ... 95
Almond Pistachio Fat Bombs (Serves 36) ... 98
Egg & Avocado Fat Bombs (Serves 5) ... 100
Apple Pie Caramel Fat Bombs (Serves 24) ... 102
Peanut Butter Chocolate Chip Cookie Dough Fat Bombs (Serves 12) ... 104
Coconut Chocolate Fat Bombs ... 106
Cinnamon Bun Fat Bombs (Serves 2) ... 108
Chocolate Drizzled Coconut Oil Fat Bombs (Serves 14) ... 110
Coconut Berry Fat Bombs ... 112
Craving Fighter Fat Bombs (Serves 32) ... 114
Cheesecake Lemon Bombs (Serves 12) ... 115
Pumpkin Pie Fat Bombs (Serves 24) ... 117
Chocolate Frozen Whips (Serves 12) ... 119
Fudge Fat Bombs (Serves 30) ... 120
Ginger Fat Bombs (Serves 10) ... 121
Cashew & Cacao Fat Bombs (Serves 20) ... 122

Pecan Pie Clusters 124
Peppermint Coffee Fat Bombs (Serves 12) 125
Key Lime Pie Fat Bombs (Serves 30) 126
Maple Almond Fudge Fat Bombs (Serves 24) 127
Mocha Ice Bombs (Serves 12) 130
Raspberry Almond Chocolate Fat Bombs (Serves 8) 131
Samoa Fudge Fat Bombs (Serves 10) 132
Sea Salt Chocolate Fat Bombs (Serves 10) 134
Blueberry Cream Fat Bombs (Serves 30) 136
Coconut Cinnamon Fat Bombs (Serves 10) 137
Sweet Treat Chocolate Fat Bombs (Serves 4) 138
Pudding Fat Bombs (Serves 6) 139
Strawberry Shortcake Keto Fat Bombs (Serves 25) 140
Coconut Orange Creamsicle Fat Bombs (Serves 10) 141
Chocolate Peanut Butter Fat Bombs (Serves 8) 142
Cookie Dough Keto Fat Bombs (Serves 30) 143
Chocolate Walnut Fat Bombs (Serves 30) 144
Everything Bagel and Lox Fat Bombs (Serves 36) 146
Ice Cream Fat Bombs (Serves 5) 147
Chocolate Chip Cookie Dough Fat Bombs (Serves 24) 148
Pumpkin Spice Fat Bombs (Serves 24) 149
Pecan Pie Fat Bombs (Serves 18) 151
White Chocolate Raspberry Fat Bombs (Serves 12) 152
Chocolate Coconut Almond Fat Bombs (Serves 30) 154
Layered Peppermint Patties Fat Bombs (Serves 24) 155
Vanilla Fat Bombs Dipped In Chocolate Fat Bombs (Serves 16) 156

Chocolate Almond Fat Bombs (Serves 15) 158

Fudge Macadamia Chocolate Fat Bombs (Serves 6) 159

Triple Layer Choconut Almond Butter Cups (Serves 12) 160

Matcha Coconut Fat Bombs (Serves 32) 163

Cardamom Orange Walnut Truffles (Serves 12) 164

Sugar-Free Maple Nut Fudge (Serves 24) 166

Sugar-Free Mounds Bars (Serves 24) 167

Vanilla Fat Bombs (Serves 14) 169

Mint Fudge Fat Bombs.. 171

Keto Fat Bomb Ice Cream (Serves 5) 172

Peppermint Mocha Fat Bombs (Serves 16)............................. 173

Blackberry Coconut Fat Bombs (Serves 16) 174

White Chocolate Coconut Fudge (Serves 24) 176

Daily Greens Fat Bomb Truffles (Serves 14) 177

White Chocolate Butter Pecan Fat Bombs (Serves 4) 179

Strawberry-Filled Coconut Fat Bombs (Serves 15) 181

No-Bake Grasshopper Bars... 182

No Bake N'oatmeal Fudge Bars (Serves 16) 184

Cinnamon Coffee Cake Collagen Fat Bombs (Serves 12) 186

Blackberry Mascarpone Fat Bombs (Serves 9) 187

Conclusion.. 189

Part 1

Introduction

This cookbook contains savory ketogenic fat bombs recipes. Keto fat bombs are low carb, but high fat snacks. Your body uses fats as the main energy source instead of glucose when you are on keto. There is no need to deprive yourself of delicious dishes and snacks if you want to lose weight or improve your health.

The keto fat bombs recipes from this cookbook will provide you with a healthy source of energy that will allow you to live your life to the fullest each day. What is more, these recipes will help you to forget about eating high-carb food and concentrate on healthier low carb dishes. This strategy is very helpful if your goal is to lose weight or strengthen your health. Keto diet helps to stay focused, decreases cholesterol level, blood pressure level or can help with the sugar level in your blood.

Many people that are on keto diet include keto fat bombs as a part of their keto diets. You can choose between savory and sweet keto fat bombs or eat both. In this book you will find only savory keto fat bombs, that are very simple to prepare and to maintain control over the nutrients and portions you consume.

Enjoy a collection of 40 savory keto fat bombs recipes that are divided into three chapters: meat keto fat bombs, fish-sea food keto fat bombs and vegetarian, plant based ketogenic bombs.

Please enjoy and test those keto bombs recipes, not always strictly following the recipes given, but adding your own flavors and ingredients!

ABOUT THE KETO DIET

The Basics of the Ketogenic Diet

The ketogenic diet is gaining popularity around the world. The latest studies have revealed that the keto diet helps you to lose your weight more effectively. Research shows a faster weight loss when participants go on a ketogenic or very low carbohydrate diet compared to patients on a more traditional low-fat diet, or even a Mediterranean diet (Campos, 2017).

"It was proven that, when you are on keto you will lose your belly faster."

What is more keto diet reduces your health risk factors. It helps to control hunger level, cholesterol level, blood pressure level, heart diseases, diabetes, epilepsy, increases your energy level and more.

Being on keto means that you will eat low carb, high fat and medium protein food. You will consume more cheeses, cream, butter, all kinds of meats and fish, oils, nuts, seeds, fresh vegetables, leafy greens, and sweeteners such as stevia, monk fruits or even erythritol.

If you eat a lot of carbs, your body will produce a lot of glucose and insulin, which eventually may lead to prediabetes and type 2 diabetes.

"More than 100 million adults in the U.S. have diabetes or prediabetes (CDC, 2017).**"**

- **Glucose** from carbohydrates is the main energy source for your body.
- **Insulin** hormone helps your body to use the glucose and enter cells.

The ketogenic puts your body into a state called ketosis. When you starve yourself or eliminate carb food and eat low carb food, your body will start producing **ketones** from the breakdown of fats in your liver that will be used as the main source of energy by your body. This state is called **ketosis**. The main aim of the ketogenic diet is to stay in this state, which will give you a lot of health benefits.

Why Go Keto?

The most visible advantage of being on keto is weight loss. When you are on a keto your body becomes more efficient in burning fat. As a result you won't feel the highs and lows that you would normally feel when consuming high carb food, because of glucose levels spiking in your blood. Eating keto dishes will help you to feel less exhausted and stabilize your mood.

Eating keto food you will see more benefits, such as:

- Loss of weight and fat - belly fat, hips fat, etc.
- Insulin level control (preventing the risk of prediabetes and type 2 diabetes)
- Improved concentration
- Optimized blood pressure
- Normalized cholesterol level
- Boosted energy level

Types of Ketogenic Diets

1) SKD – Standard Ketogenic Diet is the most common and most popular diet. This type of keto diet means, that you will eat extremely low carb (around 5%), medium protein (around 20%) and high fat (around 75%) food.
2) High Protein Ketogenic Diet is the same as SKD but contains higher amounts of protein (around 35%), less fat (around 60%), and the same amount of carbs as SKD (5%).
3) CKD – Cyclical Ketogenic Diet is less strict than SKD because you can have "free keto days" and eat high carb dishes. For example, Mondays and Wednesdays are the days when you eat high carb food, and other days of the week are the ones you consume standard keto food.
4) TKD – Targeted Ketogenic Diet is a standard keto diet with the one exception of consuming carb food around your physical exercise or training.

What Products to Eat When You Are on Keto?

There is a large variety of products you can choose to eat when you are on the ketogenic diet:

- **Meat**

You are free to choose between different types of meat, such as beef, lamb, goat, bison, chicken, turkey, duck, pork. Your diet could include hams, sausages, bacon, Jamon, Prosciutto, Salami etc.

- **Eggs**

Chicken eggs, duck eggs, goose eggs, turkey eggs, quail eggs, pheasant eggs, emu eggs.

- **Seafood**

Clam, crab, fish, lobster, octopus, oyster, shrimp, squid etc.

- **Oils and Fats**

Sunflower oil, avocado oil, olive oil, palm oil, macadamia oil, mayonnaise etc.

- **Vegetables**

You can eat leafy green ones, but also fresh as well as frozen veggies.

- **Dairy**

Butter, cream cheese, cheese, Parmesan, **Pecorino** Romano, Parmigiano Ramano, Asiago, Mozarella etc.

- **Nuts and seeds**

You can choose between different nuts and seeds like walnuts, hazelnuts, coconuts, macadamias, walnuts, sesame seeds, pumpkin seeds, sunflower seeds etc.

- **Berries**

Strawberries, raspberries, blueberries, blackberries, blackcurrants etc.

- **Sweeteners**

Stevia in drops, powder or liquid, erythritol, xylitol, monk fruit, etc.

What Products to Avoid When You Are on Keto?

- **Grains**

Oat, rice, corn, quinoa, barley, millet, amaranth grain, farro, wheat, bulgur.

- **Sugars**

Maple syrup, agave, sugar, brown sugar, honey.

- **Fruits**

Apples, apricots, bananas, oranges, kiwis, peaches.

About the keto fat bombs

What are Keto Fat Bombs?

Keto fat bombs are small snacks and could be excellent source of energy for those who are on a low carb diet. Keto fat bombs contain low amounts of carbs, but are high in fats and proteins. What is more fat bombs contain simple ingredients that you can find in every shop around the corner. Keto bombs are fast and easy to prepare or to cook. It is easy to maintain control over the nutrients and portions you consume. If you are busy during the day, but you want to eat healthy keto food and follow a ketogenic path, then eat the keto fat bombs. You can store them easily and always have few of them with you.

Main Characteristics of Savory Keto Fat Bombs

-Low carb, high fat (unsalted butter, cream)
-Small balls or mini muffins size
-Savory or spicy taste
-Stored in a refrigerator
-Contain nuts, seeds, oils
-Main ingredients: unsalted butter, cream cheese, bacon grease, seeds, spices, nuts.

Tools That We Need in Our Kitchen to Prepare Savory Fat Bombs

To prepare healthy and savory keto fat bombs you will need to have the right tools in your kitchen. The following list of tools will help you cook your savory bombs faster.

Food Scale
The food scale is the main tool in your kitchen when you are on a keto diet. It is very important because you can use it to measure any food, and it will always provide you with the same amount of food. What's more, you can use your food scale in a combination with a keto diet app that will help you to get all the data you need to eat more effectively.

Food Processor or Blender
Having a food processor or blender is critical preparing keto fat bombs recipes because it will help you to process, pulse, and blend butter, cream, oils, cheeses, nuts etc.

Electric Hand Mixer
Using an electric hand mixer will save your time and energy. It is important when you are preparing savory fat bombs, because you need to mix and combine various ingredients.

Knife Sharpening Stone
When preparing ketogenic fat bombs you often need to cut, slice or chop some ingredients. In this case, having a sharp blade will save you a lot of time and frustrations than using a dull knife.

The following chapters contain savory keto fat bombs recipes that will have your taste buds coming to life, enjoy!

Meat keto fat bombs
Lamb and Cheese Fat Bombs

Prep Time: 10 min. | Cooking Time: 55 min. | Servings: 6

Ingredients:
- 15 oz lamb, ground
- 10 oz Cheddar cheese, grated
- 6 chopped cloves of garlic
- 2 eggs
- 10 tablespoons Olive oil
- 4 tablespoons powdered garlic
- salt and pepper
- chopped dill

How to Prepare:

1. Combine the eggs, garlic, salt, pepper, powdered garlic and chopped dill with the ground lamb.
2. Add the grated Cheddar cheese and mix well and then form the lamb balls.
3. Heat the Olive oil and fry the lamb meat balls in the Olive oil for 25 minutes.
4. Sprinkle the chopped dill on top and then serve.

Nutrients per serving:
Total Carbs: 11g
Net Carbs: 7g
Total Fat: 37g
Protein: 19.9g

Calories: 189

Smoked Sausages Fat Bombs

Prep Time: 10 min. | Cooking Time: 45 min. | Servings: 4

Ingredients:
- 5 smoked sausages
- 4 eggs
- 8 oz Parmesan cheese, grated
- 1 onion, chopped
- 2 teaspoons baking powder
- 5 tablespoons unsalted butter
- 5 tablespoons Olive oil
- salt and pepper
- half teaspoon chili pepper powder
- Herbs de Provence

How to Prepare:

1. Boil the eggs for 10 minutes and then place them into the cold water for 5 minutes.
2. Heat the oil and fry the chopped onion for 10 minutes until golden brown.
3. Cut the smoked sausages and eggs into the small cubes and fry with the onion for 5 minutes more.
4. Combine all of your ingredients, except the Parmesan cheese, in a mixing bowl and mix well mashing with a fork.
5. Form the sausage balls out of the mixture and place the tasty sausages meat balls on a baking sheet.
6. Preheat the oven to 300°-320° Fahrenheit and bake the sausage balls for 20 minutes.
7. 5 minutes before the fat bombs are ready open the oven and sprinkle with the grated cheese on top.

Nutrients per serving:
Total Carbs: 9g
Net Carbs: 7g
Total Fat: 22g
Protein: 10.7g
Calories: 176

Spicy Bacon Fat Bombs

Prep Time: 5 min. | Cooking Time: 10 min. | Servings: 10

Ingredients:
- 1 seeded Cayenne pepper
- 5 oz Parmesan cheese, grated
- 10 slices smoked bacon
- 2 tablespoons bacon grease
- 10 oz cream cheese
- 10 oz unsalted butter
- 4 cloves of garlic, chopped
- 1 onion, chopped
- 4 tablespoons Olive oil
- 4 tablespoons soy sauce
- red pepper powder
- salt and pepper

How to Prepare:
1. Blend the cream cheese and butter using a food processor until they have creamy consistency.
2. Combine the diced Cayenne pepper with the cream cheese mixture, bacon grease, Olive oil, garlic, onion and spices, mashing with the fork and place the mixture in the fridge for around 2 hours.
3. Preheat the oven to 310°-320° Fahrenheit and bake the bacon slices on a baking sheet for 10 minutes.

4. Form fat balls out of the mixture and wrap the bacon slices around each ball securing it with a wooden toothpick.
5. Pour the soy sauce and sprinkle with the grated Parmesan cheese on top and then serve warm.

Tip: You can place the ketogenic fat bombs into the oven for 5-10 minutes to melt the grated Parmesan cheese.

Nutrients per serving:
Total Carbs: 10g
Net Carbs: 7g
Total Fat: 39g
Protein: 12g
Calories: 174

Chicken Breast Fat Bombs

Prep Time: 10 min. | Cooking Time: 20 min. | Servings: 6

Ingredients:
- 10 oz chicken breast
- 5 oz cream cheese
- 8 oz unsalted butter
- 4 tablespoons tomato sauce
- 7 tablespoons mayonnaise
- Herbs de Provence
- salt and pepper

How to Prepare:

1. Boil the chicken breast for 20 minutes until soft.
2. Place all of your ingredients except the tomato sauce into a food processor and then blend until they have a smooth and creamy consistency.

3. Form the chicken breast fat bombs out of the mixture and boil them for 10 minutes more and then spoon the tomato sauce.

Nutrients per serving:
Total Carbs: 8g
Net Carbs: 6g
Total Fat: 19g
Protein: 10g
Calories: 172

Smoked Bacon and Peanuts Fat Bombs

Prep Time: 10 min. |Cooking Time: 20 min. |Servings: 8

Ingredients:
- 8 smoked bacon slices
- 2 tablespoons peanuts
- 8 oz cream
- 8 oz unsalted butter
- 4 tablespoons mayonnaise
- salt and pepper
- chopped fresh chives

How to Prepare:

1. Roast the peanuts in the oven for 10 minutes until lightly browned and crispy and set aside.
2. Melt the cream and unsalted butter in a skillet for 10 minutes and then cool.

3. Combine all the ingredients except for the bacon slices and place in the fridge for 1 hour.
4. Form the balls out of the mixture and wrap the bacon slices around each ball securing it with a small wooden toothpick.
5. Add the wraps to a frying pan and fry on a low heat for about 10 minutes until light brown and then serve!

Nutrients per serving:
Total Carbs: 10g
Net Carbs: 8g
Total Fat: 38g
Protein: 19.6g
Calories: 158

Smoked Ham Fat Bombs

Prep Time: 15 min. | Cooking Time: 0 min. | Servings: 6

Ingredients:
- 10 oz smoked ham
- 5 cloves of garlic, crushed
- 2 red onions
- 5 oz cream
- 5 oz unsalted butter
- 5 oz Parmesan cheese, grated
- 2 tablespoons bacon grease
- 4 tablespoons soy sauce
- salt and pepper

How to Prepare:
1. Combine the cream, unsalted butter, crushed garlic, Parmesan cheese, bacon grease, soy sauce and spices and then blend using a food processor.
2. Cube the ham and combine all of the ingredients and mix well and then place in the fridge for 2 hours.
3. Form meat balls out of the mixture and serve.

Nutrients per serving:
Total Carbs: 10g

Net Carbs: 6g
Total Fat: 46g
Protein: 14g
Calories: 163

Bacon and Turkey Breast Fat Bombs

Prep Time: 5 min. | Cooking Time: 20 min. | Servings: 10

Ingredients:

- 10 bacon slices
- 8 oz turkey breast
- 8 oz cream
- 8 oz unsalted butter
- 5 oz Asiago cheese, cubed
- chili pepper powder
- salt and pepper
- 5 fresh basil leaves

How to Prepare:

1. Boil the water and cook the turkey breast for 20 minutes until soft and then cube it.
2. Blend the cream, unsalted butter, basil and spices using a food processor.

3. Form the fat bombs balls and press Asiago cheese cube and turkey cube inside each ball.
4. Wrap the bacon slices around each ball securing it with a wooden toothpick.

Nutrients per serving:
Total Carbs: 13g
Net Carbs: 9g
Total Fat: 37g
Protein: 21g
Calories: 234

Beef Meat Keto Fat Bombs

Prep Time: 10 min. | Cooking Time: 55 min. | Servings: 6

Ingredients:
- 15 oz beef, ground
- 6 eggs
- 8 chopped cloves of garlic
- 2 chopped onions
- 2 tablespoons Olive oil
- Herbes de Provence
- Oregano
- salt and pepper

How to Prepare:

1. Boil the eggs for 10 minutes and place them into the cold water for 5 minutes and then remove the shells from the hard-boiled eggs.

2. Combine the ground beef meat, garlic, onions, sea, pepper, Herbs de Provence and oregano mashing with a fork.
3. Coat each egg with enough of the beef mixture to cover.
4. Preheat the oven to 300°-320° Fahrenheit and sprinkle the beef fat bombs with the Olive oil and then bake them at 320°Fahrenheit for 45 minutes.
5. Serve the beef and eggs fat bombs with the sauerkraut.

Nutrients per serving:
Total Carbs: 12g
Net Carbs: 8g
Total Fat: 35g
Protein: 17g
Calories: 245

Bacon and Pecan Nuts Fat Bombs

Prep Time: 5 min. | Cooking Time: 30 min. | Servings: 6

Ingredients:
- 8 bacon slices
- 2 oz pecan nuts
- 10 oz butter, salted
- 4 cloves of garlic, chopped
- chopped chives
- salt and pepper
- Herbs de Provence

How to Prepare:
1. Roast the pecan nuts in the oven for 10 min. until lightly browned and crispy and set aside.
2. Preheat the oven to 300°-320° Fahrenheit and bake the bacon slices on a baking sheet for 20 minutes, and then crumble the bacon.
3. In a bowl, combine the butter, pecan nuts, garlic, salt, pepper, chives, Herbs de Provence and place in the fridge for 2 hours.
4. Form fat bombs out of the butter mixture and roll each fat bomb in the crumbled bacon.

Nutrients per serving:
Total Carbs: 13g
Net Carbs: 7.5g
Total Fat: 24g

Protein: 15g

Calories: 162

Chicken Livers Fat Bombs

Prep Time: 5 min. | Cooking Time: 35 min. | Servings: 6

Ingredients:
- 10 oz diced chicken livers
- 10 bacon slices
- 2 tablespoons bacon grease
- 10 oz unsalted butter
- 3 cloves of garlic, chopped
- 1 red onion, chopped
- salt and pepper
- Herbs de Provence
- chopped chives

How to Prepare:

1. Preheat the oven to 310°-320° Fahrenheit and bake the bacon slices on a baking sheet for 15 minutes and then remember to reserve the bacon grease.
2. Heat half of the butter in a frying pan and fry the onions and garlic for about 5 min. until golden.
3. Melt the remaining butter over medium heat in a pan and add the chicken livers to a pan and then cook them for 15 minutes until soft.
4. After the chicken livers are cooked transfer them, onions and garlic to a blender and pulse until they have homogeneous mass and smooth consistency.
5. Add the salt, pepper, Herbs de Provence, chives, bacon grease and mix well.
6. Place the chicken livers mixture in the fridge for around 2 hours.
7. Form fat bombs out of the mixture using a spoon, roll each chicken liver ball in the crumbled bacon and place them in the fridge for 3 hours.

Nutrients per serving:
Total Carbs: 12g
Net Carbs: 9g
Total Fat: 33g
Protein: 24g
Calories: 187

Bacon and Walnuts Fat Bombs

Prep Time: 5 min. | Cooking Time: 30 min. | Servings: 8

Ingredients:
- 10 bacon slices
- 5 oz walnuts
- 5 oz raisins
- 10 oz butter, salted
- 2 tablespoons garlic powder
- chopped parsley
- salt and pepper

How to Prepare:
1. Roast the walnuts in the oven for 10 min. until lightly browned and crispy and set aside.
2. Preheat the oven to 300°-320° Fahrenheit and bake the bacon slices on a baking sheet for 20 minutes.
3. Grind the walnuts and combine them with the raisins, butter, garlic powder, salt and pepper and then mix well mashing with a fork.
4. Place the butter mixture in the fridge for 2 hours.
5. Form fat bombs out of the butter mixture and roll each fat bomb in the bacon slices.

Nutrients per serving:

Total Carbs: 12g
Net Carbs: 8g
Total Fat: 27g
Protein: 16g

Calories: 175

Dried Plums and Bacon Fat Bombs

Prep Time: 5 min. |Cooking Time: 10 min. |Servings: 10

Ingredients:
- 10 dried plums
- 10 bacon slices
- 1 hard-boiled egg
- 8 oz unsalted butter
- 1 oz of bacon grease
- 6 tablespoons Olive oil
- 1 tablespoon mayonnaise
- 1 tablespoon soy sauce
- salt and pepper
- red pepper

How to Prepare:

1. Heat the oil and fry the bacon slices for 10 minutes over medium heat until crispy and place them on paper towels.
2. Combine the unsalted butter, boiled egg, mayonnaise, salt, pepper, red pepper and soy sauce in a mixing bowl, mashing with a fork.
3. Add the bacon grease to the fat bombs mixture stirring well and place in the fridge for 1 hour.
4. Form the fat balls out of the mixture and place the dried plum inside each ball and then wrap the bacon slices around each ball, securing it with a wooden toothpick.

Nutrients per serving:
Total Carbs: 17g
Net Carbs: 11g
Total Fat: 45g
Protein: 28g
Calories: 179

Bacon and Parmesan Cheese Fat Bombs

Prep Time: 5 min. | Cooking Time: 20 min. | Servings: 10

Ingredients:
- 10 bacon slices
- 10 oz Parmesan cheese, cubed
- 10 oz unsalted butter
- chili pepper powder
- salt and pepper
- fresh parsley

How to Prepare:

1. Preheat the oven to 300°-320° Fahrenheit and bake the bacon slices on a baking sheet for 20 minutes.
2. Blend the unsalted butter, parsley and spices using a food processor until smooth and creamy consistency.
3. Form the fat bombs balls and press Parmesan cheese cube inside each ball.
4. Wrap the bacon slices around each ball securing it with a wooden toothpick.

Nutrients per serving:
Total Carbs: 12g
Net Carbs: 8g

Total Fat: 38g
Protein: 24g
Calories: 247

Grilled Fat Bombs

Prep Time: 5 min. | Cooking Time: 25 min. | Servings: 10

Ingredients:
- 10 raw meat sausages
- 10 oz cream
- 10 oz unsalted butter
- 5 oz Piave cheese, grated
- 7 tablespoons mayonnaise
- 5 fresh basil leaves
- Herbs de Provence
- salt and pepper

How to Prepare:
1. Cut the raw meat sausages into small pieces.

2. Melt the unsalted butter for 10 minutes and blend with the cream using a food processor until they have creamy consistency.
3. Combine and mix well the sausages with all of the ingredients except the cheese.
4. Form 10 sausage balls out of the mixture and grill them for 15 minutes and then sprinkle with the Piave cheese and serve!

Nutrients per serving:
Total Carbs: 8.5g
Net Carbs: 5g
Total Fat: 36g
Protein: 15g
Calories: 178

Salami Fat Bombs

Prep Time: 5 min. | Cooking Time: 15 min. | Servings: 6

Ingredients:

- 10 oz salami
- 5 cloves of garlic, crushed
- 1 onion
- 10 oz unsalted butter
- 5 oz Cheddar cheese, grated
- 4 tablespoons mayonnaise
- 2 tablespoons Olive oil
- salt and pepper

How to Prepare:

1. Heat the oil and fry the onion on low heat for 10 minutes until caramelized.
2. Cube the salami and fry with the chopped onion for 5 minutes more.
3. Combine the unsalted butter, crushed garlic, Cheddar cheese, mayonnaise and spices and then blend using a food processor.
4. Combine the salami and onion with the butter mixture and mix well with a fork and then place in the fridge for 2 hours.
5. Form salami balls out of the mixture and serve.

Nutrients per serving:
Total Carbs: 9g
Net Carbs: 6g
Total Fat: 36g
Protein: 22g

Calories: 159

Fish and seafood keto fat bombs
Mackerel Fat Bombs

Prep Time: 10 min. | Cooking Time: 10 min. | Servings: 6

Ingredients:
- 1 smoked mackerel
- 2 fresh zucchini's
- 6 oz unsalted butter
- 6 oz cream cheese
- 4 cloves of garlic, chopped
- 4 tablespoons Olive oil
- 1 tablespoon soy sauce
- salt and pepper
- basil

How to Prepare:
1. Cut the fresh zucchinis into the longitudinal strips.

2. Heat the Olive oil and fry the zucchinis strips for 10 minutes over low heat from both sides (5 minutes each side).
3. Blend the mackerel meat, cream cheese, butter, soy sauce, salt and pepper until smooth consistency and place in the fridge for 30 minutes.
4. Form the mackerel fat bombs out of the mixture and roll each bomb in the zucchini slices, adding the chopped garlic and basil on top.

Nutrients per serving:
Total Carbs: 9g
Net Carbs: 7g
Total Fat: 24g
Protein: 13g
Calories: 149

Mackerel and Lemon Fat Bombs

Prep Time: 10 min. | Cooking Time: 0 min. | Servings: 6

Ingredients:
- 2 smoked mackerels
- 8 oz cream
- 8 oz unsalted butter
- 7 tablespoons mayonnaise
- 5 tablespoons sunflower oil
- salt and pepper
- chopped dill
- squeezed lemon juice

How to Prepare:
1. Blend the cream and unsalted butter using a food processor until they have a creamy and smooth consistency.
2. Cut the smoked mackerels meat into pieces and mix all of the ingredients except for the dill and place in the fridge for 1 hour.
3. Form fish balls out of the mixture and sprinkle the chopped dill on top and then pour the lemon juice and you are free to serve!

Nutrients per serving:

Total Carbs: 8g
Net Carbs: 6g
Total Fat: 32g
Protein: 21g
Calories: 163

Sardines Fat Bombs

Prep Time: 10 min. | Cooking Time: 0 min. | Servings: 12

Ingredients:
- 2 cans of drained sardines
- 5 oz Cheddar cheese, grated
- 5 oz unsalted butter
- 5 oz cream cheese
- 5 cloves of garlic, chopped
- 5 tablespoons mayonnaise
- 12 cucumber slices
- chopped chives

How to Prepare:

1. Blend the sardines, cream cheese and unsalted butter using a food processor until they have creamy consistency.
2. In a mixing bowl, combine the mixture with the grated Cheddar cheese, garlic and mayonnaise

mashing with a fork and then place in the fridge for around 1 hour.
3. Form 12 fat bombs out of the sardine mixture.
4. Then grill the fat bombs, cool and add the chopped chives on top.

Nutrients per serving:
Total Carbs: 7.9g
Net Carbs: 6g
Total Fat: 21g
Protein: 14.2g
Calories: 162

Sea Perch Fat Bombs

Prep Time: 10 min. | Cooking Time: 0 min. | Servings: 2

Ingredients:
- 1 smoked sea perch
- 5 cloves of garlic, chopped
- 7 tablespoons mayonnaise
- 4 tablespoons unsalted butter
- 4 tablespoons Olive oil
- salt and pepper
- fresh chopped greenery

How to Prepare:
1. Mash the smoked sea perch meat with a fork.
2. Combine the smoked sea perch meat with all of your ingredients and mash well with a fork and then place in the fridge for 1 hour.
3. Form the fat bombs out of the mixture and serve them.

Nutrients per serving:
Total Carbs: 12g
Net Carbs: 9g
Total Fat: 39g
Protein: 27g

Calories: 131

Crab Meat Fat Bombs

Prep Time: 10 min. | Cooking Time: 35 min. | Servings: 6

Ingredients:
- 10 oz of crab meat
- 7 oz cream
- 7 oz unsalted butter
- 4 cloves of garlic, chopped
- 4 oz Mozzarella cheese, cubed
- 5 tablespoons mayonnaise
- 1 teaspoon mustard
- 1 egg
- 3 oz breadcrumbs

- 7 tablespoons sunflower oil
- salt and pepper

How to Prepare:

1. Melt the unsalted butter and cream in a skillet.
2. Boil the crab meat for 15 minutes until soft and pulse using a blender.
3. Mix all of the ingredients except the Mozzarella cheese, egg, breadcrumbs, oil and place in the fridge for 30 minutes.
4. Form 6 balls out of the mixture and place the Mozzarella cheese cubes inside each ball.
5. Beat the egg and dip each crab ball in the egg and roll the crab bombs in breadcrumbs.
6. Fry the crab balls in the sunflower oil for 20 minutes until light golden and crisp.

Nutrients per serving:
Total Carbs: 8g
Net Carbs: 6.8g
Total Fat: 25g
Protein: 19g
Calories: 129

Salmon and Cucumber Fat Bombs

Prep Time: 5 min. | Cooking Time: 0 min. | Servings: 6

Ingredients:
- 8 oz smoked salmon
- 1 fresh cucumber
- 7 oz cream cheese
- 5 oz unsalted butter
- 4 oz Pecorino Romano cheese, grated
- 3 tablespoon white wine vinegar
- chopped fresh parsley
- salt

How to Prepare:
1. Combine the cream cheese and butter in a mixing bowl, mashing with a fork until creamy consistency.
2. Peel the cucumber and cube it and then cube the smoked salmon.
3. Combine all of the ingredients and pour the white wine vinegar and mix well.
4. Place the salmon mixture in the fridge for 50 minutes.
5. Form 12 fish balls out of the mixture and serve.

Nutrients per serving:
Total Carbs: 13g
Net Carbs: 9g

Total Fat: 29g
Protein: 20g
Calories: 102

Tuna and Salmon Fat Bombs

Prep Time: 5 min. | Cooking Time: 30 min. | Servings: 6

Ingredients:
- 8 oz smoked salmon
- 1 can of tuna in oil
- 7 oz unsalted butter
- 4 cloves of garlic, chopped
- 4 tablespoons mayonnaise
- 4 tablespoon soy sauce
- chopped dill
- Herbs de Provence
- salt and pepper

How to Prepare:
1. Cut the smoked salmon into pieces and place it into a food processor.

2. Add the tuna, unsalted butter, garlic, mayonnaise, soy sauce, salt, pepper, Herbs de Provence and blend until smooth.
3. Form 12 fat bombs out of the fish mixture and place them in the fridge for few hours.
4. Serve the tuna-salmon fat bombs with the chopped dill on top.

Tip: You can sprinkle freshly squeezed lemon juice on top!

Nutrients per serving:
Total Carbs: 11g
Net Carbs: 8g
Total Fat: 29g
Protein: 19g
Calories: 168

Pacific Halibut Fat Bombs

Prep Time: 10 min. | Cooking Time: 0 min. | Servings: 6

Ingredients:
- 5 oz pacific halibut, hot smoked
- 6 avocado halves, pitted
- 6 cloves of garlic, crushed
- 7 tablespoons mayonnaise
- salt and pepper
- fresh chopped chives

How to Prepare:
1. Mash the smoked halibut meat with a fork.
2. Combine the smoked halibut meat with all of your ingredients except for the avocado and mix well and then place in the fridge for 1 hour.
3. Fill the avocado halves with the halibut mixture and sprinkle the chopped chives on top.

Nutrients per serving:
Total Carbs: 11g
Net Carbs: 6g
Total Fat: 31g
Protein: 24g
Calories: 138

Crème Fat Bombs

Prep Time: 10 min. | Cooking Time: 10 min. | Servings: 12

Ingredients:
- 10 smoked salmon slices
- 8 oz cream
- 5 oz unsalted butter
- 2 onions, chopped
- 8 tablespoons mayonnaise
- 12 organic unsalted crackers
- 2 tablespoons pumpkin seeds oil
- 1 tablespoon soy sauce
- salt and pepper
- oregano
- chopped chives

How to Prepare:

1. Melt the butter for 10 minutes and combine it with the cream in a mixing bowl, mashing with a fork until smooth.
2. Add the onions, mayonnaise, pumpkin seeds oil, soy sauce, salt, pepper and oregano and mix well using a hand mixer.
3. The mixture should be placed in the fridge for around 1 hour.
4. Place the creamy mixture on organic unsalted crackers, adding the smoked salmon slices and the chopped chives on top.

Nutrients per serving:
Total Carbs: 9g
Net Carbs: 6g
Total Fat: 25g
Protein: 13g
Calories: 139

Herrings Fat Bombs

Prep Time: 10 min. | Cooking Time: 0 min. | Servings: 8

Ingredients:

- 2 smoked herrings
- 8 avocado halves, pitted
- 4 oz fresh celery, chopped
- 1 red onion, chopped
- 5 cloves of garlic, crushed
- 6 tablespoons mayonnaise
- 4 teaspoons lemon juice
- salt and pepper

How to Prepare:

1. Mash the smoked herring meat with a fork.
2. Combine the smoked herring meat with all of your ingredients except for the avocado and mix well and then place in the fridge for 1 hour.
3. Fill the avocado halves with the herring mixture and pour the lemon juice on top.

Nutrients per serving:
Total Carbs: 10g
Net Carbs: 6g
Total Fat: 29g

Protein: 19g
Calories: 145

Tuna and Caviar Fat Bombs

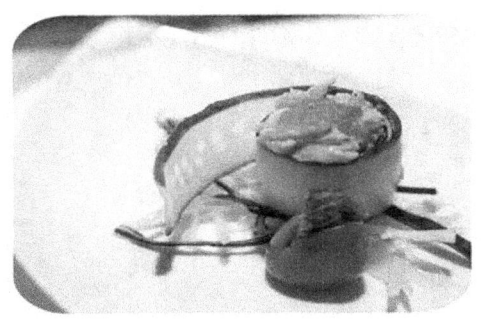

Prep Time: 10 min. | Cooking Time: 10 min. | Servings: 2

Ingredients:
- 1 can of tuna in oil
- 2 tablespoons caviar
- 1 long cucumber (ex. Bologna)
- 2 cloves of garlic, chopped
- 7 tablespoons mayonnaise
- salt and pepper
- Herbes de Provence
- chopped dill

How to Prepare:

1. Cut the cucumber into the longitudinal strips and sprinkle with the salt and pepper.

2. Combine the tuna, garlic, mayonnaise and spices, mashing with a fork until creamy consistency.
3. Form the fat bombs out of the mixture and spoon them inside each cucumber roll.
4. Place teaspoon of caviar on top and sprinkle with the chopped dill to serve.

Nutrients per serving:
Total Carbs: 11g
Net Carbs: 7g
Total Fat: 25g
Protein: 17g

Calories: 133

Tuna and Zucchini Fat Bombs

Prep Time: 10 min. | Cooking Time: 15 min. | Servings: 6

Ingredients:
- 1 can of tuna in oil
- 1 small and young zucchini
- 3 eggs
- 4 cloves of garlic, chopped

- 1 tablespoon soy sauce
- 2 tablespoons Olive oil
- salt and pepper
- powdered red pepper
- chopped dill

How to Prepare:

1. Boil the eggs for 15 minutes and then halve them and scoop out the egg yolks.
2. Blend the egg yolks, tuna and the remaining ingredients in your food processor until they have smooth consistency.
3. Slice the zucchini into 8 rings and sprinkle with the salt and red pepper.
4. Form 8 fat bombs out of the mixture and place them on the zucchini slices and sprinkle the chopped dill on top.

Nutrients per serving:
Total Carbs: 9g
Net Carbs: 6g
Total Fat: 26g
Protein: 18g

Calories: 149

Spicy Shrimps Fat Bombs

Prep Time: 10 min. | Cooking Time: 15 min. | Servings: 4

Ingredients:
- 8 eggs
- 8 oz shrimps, frozen
- 2 teaspoons chili pepper powder
- 8 oz Parmesan cheese, grated
- 4 crushed cloves of garlic
- 8 tablespoons mayonnaise
- 4 tablespoons Olive oil
- salt and pepper
- fresh chives, chopped

How to Prepare:

1. Boil the shrimps and eggs for 15 minutes.

2. Halve the eggs and scoop out the egg yolks into a bowl.
3. Combine the grated Parmesan cheese with all of your ingredients except for the shrimps, egg halves and chives.
4. Fill the egg halves with the Parmesan mixture and add the boiled shrimps and chopped chives on top.

Nutrients per serving:
Total Carbs: 8g
Net Carbs: 6g
Total Fat: 25g
Protein: 16g
Calories: 147

Mackerel and Eggs Fat Bombs

Prep Time: 10 min. | Cooking Time: 15 min. | Servings: 4

Ingredients:
- 1 smoked mackerel
- 5 eggs
- 5 oz grated Cheddar cheese
- 5 crushed cloves of garlic
- 8 tablespoons mayonnaise
- salt and pepper
- Herbs de Provence
- chopped celery

How to Prepare:

1. Boil the eggs for 15 minutes, cool them and then halve them and scoop out the egg yolks into a bowl.
2. Combine the mackerel meat with all of your ingredients except the egg halves and celery. Blend the mackerel mixture using a food processor until it has the smooth consistency.
3. Fill the egg halves with the mackerel mixture and sprinkle the chopped celery on top and then serve.

Nutrients per serving:
Total Carbs: 8g
Net Carbs: 5g

Total Fat: 34g
Protein: 22g
Calories: 147

Shrimps Fat Bombs

Prep Time: 5 min. | Cooking Time: 15 min. | Servings: 6

Ingredients:
- 8 oz shrimps, frozen
- 8 oz unsalted butter
- 4 tablespoons mayonnaise
- 4 tablespoon soy sauce
- chopped dill
- Herbs de Provence
- salt and pepper

How to Prepare:
1. Boil the shrimps for 15 minutes until soft.
2. Place the shrimps with the unsalted butter, mayonnaise, soy sauce, dill, salt, pepper and Herbs de Provence into a food processor and blend until smooth.
3. Form the fat bombs out of the mixture and place them in the fridge for 3 hours.
4. Serve the shrimps fat bombs with the vegetable salad.

Nutrients per serving:
Total Carbs: 9g

Net Carbs: 6g
Total Fat: 27g
Protein: 18g
Calories: 148

Vegetable keto fat bombs
Cucumber and Tomato Fat Bombs

Prep Time: 5 min. | Cooking Time: 0 min. | Servings: 2

Ingredients:

- 1 cucumber
- 2 tomatoes
- 7 tablespoons cream
- 4 tablespoons unsalted butter
- 1 oz grated Cheddar cheese
- 1 oz chopped chives
- 2 chopped cloves of garlic
- salt and pepper
- chopped dill

How to Prepare:

1. Combine the cream and butter and blend using a food processor.
2. Peel and grate the cucumber and then combine the Cheddar cheese, chives and garlic with the cream mixture and add the spices.
3. Cut a slice from the top of each tomato and discard the seeds and juice with the spoon.
4. Fill each tomato with the delicious cream and cheese mixture and sprinkle the chopped dill on top.
5. Place the tomato fat bombs into the fridge for 2 hours and serve.

Nutrients per serving:
Total Carbs: 15g
Net Carbs: 11g
Total Fat: 18g
Protein: 6.9g
Calories: 113

Spicy Peanuts Fat Bombs

Prep Time: 5 min. | Cooking Time: 10 min. | Servings: 5

Ingredients:
- 1 tablespoon chili pepper powder
- 2 tablespoons peanuts
- 8 oz unsalted butter
- 8 teaspoons sesame seeds
- 2 tablespoons sesame oil
- 5 teaspoons garlic powder
- salt and pepper

How to Prepare:
1. Roast the peanuts and sesame seeds in the oven for 10 min. until lightly browned and crispy and set aside.
2. Combine the unsalted butter, peanuts, sesame oil, salt, pepper, chili pepper, garlic powder and mix well and then place in the fridge for around 2 hours.
3. Form the fat bombs out of the mixture using a spoon and roll each fat bomb in the toasted sesame seeds and serve or store in the fridge.

Nutrients per serving:
Total Carbs: 8g

Net Carbs: 6g
Total Fat: 26g
Protein: 18g
Calories: 99

Garlic and Cheese Fat Bombs

Prep Time: 5 min. | *Cooking Time: 0 min.* | *Servings: 6*

Ingredients:

- 7 oz Parmesan cheese, grated
- 5 cloves of garlic, chopped
- 7 tablespoons mayonnaise
- 5 teaspoons soy sauce
- 2 tablespoons pumpkin seeds, ground
- Herbs de Provence
- salt and pepper

How to Prepare:

1. In a bowl, combine the Parmesan cheese with the garlic, mayonnaise, soy sauce and spices and then mix well.
2. Place the cheesy mixture into the fridge for 3 hours.

3. Form cheese fat bombs out of the mixture and sprinkle the ground pumpkin seeds on top.

Nutrients per serving:
Total Carbs: 9.4g
Net Carbs: 4.9g
Total Fat: 21g
Protein: 16g

Calories: 98

Sunflower Seeds Fat Bombs

Prep Time: 5 min. | Cooking Time: 20 min. | Servings: 6

Ingredients:
- 8 oz sunflower seeds
- 6 oz cream cheese
- 6 oz unsalted butter
- 5 oz grated Parmesan cheese
- 5 oz fresh spinach
- 4 tablespoons sunflower oil
- 2 oz peanuts

How to Prepare:
1. Toast the sunflower seeds for 10 minutes until lightly browned.
2. Then roast the peanuts in the oven for 10 minutes until lightly browned and crispy and set aside.
3. Combine the cream cheese and butter in a mixing bowl, mashing with a fork.
4. Chop the spinach and pour the sunflower oil on top.
5. Combine all of the ingredients and place in the fridge for 1 hour.
6. Form the fat bombs out of the mixture and serve.

Nutrients per serving:

Total Carbs: 9g
Net Carbs: 5g
Total Fat: 29g
Protein: 19g
Calories: 109

Fried Brie Cheese Fat Bombs

Prep Time: 5 min. | Cooking Time: 20 min. | Servings: 10

Ingredients:
- 8 oz Brie cheese, chopped
- 2 onions, chopped
- 5 oz cream cheese
- 5 oz unsalted butter
- 2 teaspoons garlic powder
- salt and pepper
- Herbes de Provence
- chopped fresh celery

How to Prepare:

1. Blend the cream cheese, butter and Brie Cheese using a food processor.
2. Heat the oil and fry the onions for 10 minutes until golden brown.
3. Combine the Brie cheese mixture with the onions, celery, garlic powder and spices.
4. Form the fat bombs out of the mixture and fry them in oil for 10 minutes and then serve.

Nutrients per serving:
Total Carbs: 11g
Net Carbs: 8g
Total Fat: 22g
Protein: 15g
Calories: 95

Tomatoes Fat Bombs

Prep Time: 5 min. | *Cooking Time: 0 min.* | *Servings: 4*

Ingredients:
- 8 cherry tomatoes
- 8 oz cream cheese
- 8 oz unsalted butter
- 5 oz Cheddar cheese
- 3 tablespoons mayonnaise
- 6 chopped cloves of garlic
- salt and pepper
- Herbs de Provence
- chopped dill

How to Prepare:

1. Blend the cream cheese, butter, garlic and spices using a food processor.
2. Halve the tomatoes and cube the Cheddar cheese and then combine with the other ingredients in a mixing bowl, mashing with a fork and place in the fridge for 1 hour.
3. Form the tomatoes balls out of the mixture, sprinkle with the chopped dill and serve.

Nutrients per serving:

Total Carbs: 11g
Net Carbs: 7g
Total Fat: 39g
Protein: 24g

Calories: 115

Pumpkin Seeds Fat Bombs

Prep Time: 5 min. | Cooking Time: 10 min. | Servings: 4

Ingredients:
- 8 oz unsalted butter
- 4 teaspoons pumpkin seeds
- 4 tablespoons pumpkin seeds oil
- half teaspoon chili flakes
- half teaspoon garlic powder
- 2 teaspoons shredded coconut
- salt and pepper

How to Prepare:

1. Toast the pumpkin seeds for 10 minutes and then pulse the seeds using a blender.

2. Mix all of the ingredients except the shredded coconut and place in the fridge for 40 minutes.
3. Form the fat bombs out of the mixture and roll the balls in the shredded coconut and serve.

Nutrients per serving:
Total Carbs: 8g
Net Carbs: 6g
Total Fat: 23g
Protein: 17g

Calories: 147

Dried Tomatoes Fat Bombs

Prep Time: 5 min. | Cooking Time: 10 min. | Servings: 10

Ingredients:
- 7 oz sundried tomatoes
- 7 oz cream
- 7 oz unsalted butter
- 1 onion
- 7 oz Feta cheese, cubed
- 5 oz fresh spinach

How to Prepare:
1. Combine the cream and butter in a mixing bowl, mashing with a fork and then blend using a hand mixer or a food processor.
2. Chop the dried tomatoes and onion.
3. Mix all of the ingredients and place in the fridge for 1 hour.
4. Form 10 fat bombs out of the mixture and serve.

Nutrients per serving:
Total Carbs: 10g
Net Carbs: 7g
Total Fat: 26g
Protein: 20g

Calories: 123

Pumpkin Fat Bombs

Prep Time: 5 min. | Cooking Time: 20 min. | Servings: 6

Ingredients:
- 1 cup pumpkin puree
- 4 oz pecan nuts
- 5 oz cream
- 5 oz unsalted butter
- salt and pepper

How to Prepare:

1. Roast the pecan nuts in the oven for 10 minutes until lightly browned and crispy and then set aside.
2. Grind half of the pecan nuts and melt the cream with butter for 10 minutes.
3. Combine all of the ingredients in a mixing bowl and spoon the mixture into the silicone molds and then top with pecan nuts.
4. Freeze for 2 hours and you are free to serve.

Nutrients per serving:
Total Carbs: 11g
Net Carbs: 7g
Total Fat: 28g
Protein: 19g
Calories: 109

Spicy Chili and Coconut Fat Bombs

Prep Time: 5 min. | Cooking Time: 10 min. | Servings: 8

Ingredients:
- 7 oz unsalted butter
- 7 oz coconut oil
- half teaspoon chili pepper
- half teaspoon cayenne pepper
- salt and pepper

How to Prepare:
1. Melt the unsalted butter and coconut oil in a pan over low heat.
2. Mix in the chili pepper, cayenne pepper, salt and pepper and mix all the ingredients well and then cool the mixture.

3. Pour the mixture into 8 small paper muffin cups or candy cups and place in the fridge for around few hours.

Nutrients per serving:
Total Carbs: 9g
Net Carbs: 6g
Total Fat: 19g
Protein: 15g
Calories: 172

Conclusion

Thank you and I hope you have enjoyed savory keto fat bombs cookbook.

This collection of savory keto fat bombs recipes will have a positive impact on your health and body. Keto diet will lead you to a higher energy level. The ketogenic diet could help you to maintain the right weight without starving yourself. But remember! Before you start, it is always a good idea to consult your doctor about your plans.

Part 2

Introduction

I hope you like all the recipes I've included. There are so many great fat bombs to try out on the keto diet. These quick and easy recipes should help get you started off on the right foot. Whether you like things savory or sweet this recipe guide has you covered.

Let's begin!

Chapter 1: what is a keto fat bomb?

What Constitutes A Keto Fat Bomb?

1. Fat bombs are either sweet or savory. You'll find more recipes that swing towards the sweet side but there are plenty of savory recipe options available. A lot of the sweeter recipes call for stevia, a lower calorie and no-carb sweetener. Many of the savory fat bombs are made with items like bacon, chicken, sausage, or salmon.

2. Fat bombs are small in size. These items are high in fat so they are meant to be eaten in smaller-sized servings. They will normally take the shape of miniature muffins or a smaller-sized ball.

3. Fat bombs can be made in larger batches and stored in the refrigerator or freezer. Many fat bomb recipes make 10 or more servings at a time. Ideal for people who want to cook once or twice a week and still have healthy options on hand throughout the week. Fat bombs contain a high amount of fat and therefore will need to be kept cold when being stored. These items are not meant to sit at room temperature for long periods. Fat bombs can usually last for between 1 to 2 weeks when stored properly.

4. Fat bombs are high in healthy fats. These healthy fats are important when following a keto diet because

they help to lower the levels of inflammation in the body. Many keto fat bombs will have some form of coconut butter or coconut oil in them. These oils also help to solidify the fat bombs and therefore make them less of a mess to eat.

5. Fat bombs will often have seeds or nuts. Nuts are only meant to be eaten in small amounts due to the number of carbohydrates they contain. This makes them ideal for fat bombs. Peanuts are not technically nuts so the keto diet substitutes peanut butter with almond butter in their recipes.

3 General Ingredients In Fat Bomb Recipes

1. Healthy Fats - These include coconut milk, coconut oil, coconut cream, bacon fat, butter, ghee, cacao butter, avocado oil.

2. Flavoring - These include cacao powder, peppermint, sugar-free vanilla extract, salt, dark chocolate, and spices.

3. Texture - These include pecans, cacao nibs, bacon bits, almonds, shredded coconut, chia seeds, and walnuts.

3 Steps For Making Fat Bombs

1. Mix each of your ingredients together in your mixing bowl, blender, or processor. Melt any solids that need to become liquid.

2. Form your fat bombs by hand or pour your mixture into a baking pan or muffin cups.

3. Freeze or refrigerate your fat bombs for a few hours until the mixture solidifies. Cut your fat bombs into slices if you made them in a baking pan.

Chapter 2: sweet keto fat bomb recipes

In this section, I will show you 75+ sweet ketogenic fat bomb recipes you can cook for yourself. These are keto fat bombs are geared towards people wanting to satisfy their sweet tooth. These are easy to prepare no matter what your level in the kitchen. These tasty treats will help keep you on track with your ketogenic diet.

Almond Joy Fat Bombs (Serves 12)

Ingredients:

Coconut Filling:

1 cup of Unsweetened Coconut Flakes

2 tablespoons of Coconut Oil

1/4 cup of Unsweetened Coconut Milk

1/2 teaspoon of Almond Extract

1/4 teaspoon of Xanthan Gum

20 drops of Liquid Stevia

Chocolate Coating:

4 tablespoons of Coconut Oil

2 ounces of Unsweetened Bakers Chocolate

12 Almonds

20 drops of Liquid Stevia

Directions:

Coconut Filling:

1. Heat your saucepan over a low heat and add your coconut milk to your pan.

2. Add your coconut flakes and coconut oil, and stir allowing it to cook down a little.

3. Add the stevia drops and your almond extract. Stir and allow it to cook on low for approximately 5 minutes.

4. Add your xanthan gum and stir.

5. Line your 8x4 loaf pan with parchment paper and pour your coconut mixture into your pan. Press it out evenly over your parchment paper (1/2 inch thick) and allow it to set in the fridge for 1 hour.

6. Pull out your parchment paper and cut your coconut bar into 12 even-sized pieces.

7. Optional: Place your almond on top and press down gently into the center.

8. Place your almond joys in the freezer as you make your chocolate coating.

Chocolate Coating:

1. Chop your chocolate up and add to your microwave safe bowl.

2. Add your stevia and coconut oil to the bowl and microwave until fully melted.

3. Pull your almond joys out of the freezer and dip them into your chocolate coating either partially or fully coating them.

4. Keep stored in your refrigerator.

5. Serve and Enjoy!

Nutrition Facts:

Calories: 140.5

Calories from Fat: 128

Net Carbs: 1.5 grams

Almond Pistachio Fat Bombs (Serves 36)

Ingredients:

1 cup of Creamy Coconut Butter

1 cup of Coconut Oil (Firm)

1/2 cup of Finely Chopped & Melted Cacao Butter

1/4 cup of Chopped Raw Shelled Pistachios

1 cup of All-Natural Roasted Almond Butter

1/2 cup of Full Fat Coconut Milk (Chilled)

2 teaspoons of Chai Spice

1 tablespoon of Pure Vanilla Extract

1/4 cup of Ghee

1/4 teaspoon of Pure Almond Extract

1/4 teaspoon of Himalayan Salt

Directions:

1. Grease and line your 9-inch square baking pan with parchment paper. Leave some on a side for easier unmolding. Set to the side.

2. Melt your cacao butter in your small-sized saucepan set over a low heat, stirring often. Reserve.

3. Add all of your ingredients, except for shelled pistachios and cacao butter, to a large-sized mixing bowl. Mix with your hand mixer, starting on low speed and progressively moving higher until all of your ingredients are well combined and your mixture becomes airy and light.

4. Pour your melted cacao butter right into your almond mixture and mix on low speed until it's all incorporated.

5. Transfer to your prepared pan, spread as evenly as you can and sprinkle with your chopped pistachios.

6. Refrigerate until set, at least 4 hours but preferably overnight.

7. Cut into 36 even sized squares.

8. Serve and Enjoy!

Nutrition Facts:

Calories: 170

Calories from Fat: 157

Egg & Avocado Fat Bombs (Serves 5)

Ingredients:

1/2 Peeled Large Avocado (Seeds Removed)

3 Large Cooked Egg Yolks

1/4 cup of Mayonnaise

1/2 teaspoon of Salt

1 tablespoon of Lime or Lemon Juice

2 tablespoons of Chopped Spring Onions or Chives

Freshly Ground Black Pepper

Directions:

1. Cook your eggs.

2. Fill your small-sized saucepan with water up to three quarters. Add a pinch of salt. This will stop your eggs from cracking. Bring to a boil. Using your spoon or hand, dip each of your eggs in and out of the boiling water. This will stop your eggs from cracking as the temperature change won't be so sudden. To get your eggs hard-boiled it should take approximately 10 minutes. This timing works well for large-sized eggs. Once finished, remove from the heat and place in your bowl filled with cold water. When your eggs are chilled, peel off their shells.

3. Halve your avocado and remove the seeds and peel. Cut your eggs in half and carefully - without breaking your egg whites - spoon your egg yolks into a bowl.

4. Place your cut up avocado into your food processor and add your egg yolks, lemon juice, mayonnaise, pepper, and salt. Process until smooth. Alternatively, mash with your fork until creamy and well combined.

5. Serve with cucumber slices and spring onion on top, or fill up your egg white halves and make deviled eggs. To avoid browning, store in an airtight container and keep for a maximum of 5 days.

6. Enjoy!

Nutrition Facts:

Calories: 147

Net Carbs: 1.1 grams

Apple Pie Caramel Fat Bombs (Serves 24)

Ingredients:

2 Sliced & Cored Medium Organic Green Apples

2 tablespoons of Coconut Oil

1 teaspoon of Cinnamon

5.4 ounces of Coconut Cream

20 drops of English Toffee Stevia

1/2 cup of Coconut Butter

Pinch of Sea Salt

Directions:

1. In your skillet, saute your apples in the coconut oils until soft.

2. Add your cinnamon and stir to coat.

3. In your high-powered blender, combine the rest of your ingredients and blend on high until liquefied.

4. Pour into your silicone molds.

5. Place into your freezer until firm.

6. Pop out of your molds and store in a plastic bag in your refrigerator.

7. Serve and Enjoy!

Nutrition Facts:

Calories: 67

Carbs: 2.7 grams

Peanut Butter Chocolate Chip Cookie Dough Fat Bombs (Serves 12)

Ingredients:

6 ounces of Softened Cream Cheese

6 tablespoons of Softened Butter

3 tablespoons of Gentle Sweet (Equivalent of 1/4 cup of Sugar)

1 teaspoon of Vanilla Extract

6 scoops of Powdered MCT Oil

1/4 cup of Lily's Chocolate Chips

1/2 cup of Peanut Butter

Directions:

1. Combine your cream cheese, butter, cream cheese, vanilla extract, sweetener, and peanut butter in a bowl using your hand mixer. Mix them until well combined.

2. Stir in your chocolate chips. Cover and freeze for approximately 10 minutes.

3. Remove your bowl from your freezer and use a cookie scoop to scoop cookie dough onto a wax-paper lined dish.

4. Place your cookie dough balls back in the freezer for approximately 20 to 30 minutes, until firm.

5. Once frozen, remove your fat bombs from the freezer and place in a Ziploc bag or container. Store in your freezer until you're ready to eat.

6. Serve and Enjoy!

Nutrition Facts:

Calories: 214

Carbs: 6 grams

Coconut Chocolate Fat Bombs

Ingredients:

1/2 cup of Cocoa Powder

2 cups of Virgin Coconut Oil (Soft but Still Solid)

2 teaspoons of Vanilla Extract

6 tablespoons of Raw Honey

Dash of Salt (More to Taste)

Directions:

1. Add your cocoa powder, coconut oil, vanilla extract, honey, and salt to your food processor. Process until all of your ingredients are mixed evenly, stopping your food processor once or twice to scrape down the sides.

2. Taste your mixture to be sure that the flavor is to your liking. If desired, you can additional salt or honey as needed.

3. If using silicone molds, you want your coconut oil mixture to be pourable. If it's too thick, it's harder to fill your molds. You can process for longer to make your mixture thinner.

4. If you are not using molds, pick a flat surface that will fit in your freezer, such as a cutting board, and line it with your parchment paper. You want your mixture to

be thicker and more solid, so it can be dropped onto your surface in individual dollops and won't run. If needed, you can put your food processor in the fridge for a couple of minutes to harden your mixture.

5. If using silicone molds, lay out your molds on your cutting board, then use your ladle to fill all of your molds with the coconut oil mixture.

6. If using a surface lined with parchment paper, use your spoon to drop dollops of your mixture onto your surface.

7. Transfer molds or surface to your freezer and freeze until your fat bombs become solid.

8. Pop them out and store in a lidded container in your freezer. Repeat this process until all of your fat bombs have been frozen.

9. These will keep in your freezer indefinitely. You can also store them in the refrigerator. Do not leave these at room temperature for more than a few minutes. Coconut oil melts at 76 degrees and these will get soft.

10. Serve and Enjoy!

Cinnamon Bun Fat Bombs (Serves 2)

Ingredients:

1/8 teaspoon of Cinnamon

1/2 cup of Unsweetened Creamed Coconut (Cut Into Chunks)

1st Icing:

1 tablespoon of Extra Virgin Coconut Oil (Not Melted)

1 tablespoon of Almond Butter

2nd Icing:

1/2 teaspoon of Cinnamon

1 tablespoon of Extra Virgin Coconut Oil or Almond Butter

Directions:

1. Line your dish or pan with appropriate liners.

2. In your bowl, using your hands, mix your cinnamon and coconut cream. Pat into the dish. Fills 2 mini loaf sections.

3. First Icing: In a different bowl using your whisk, whisk together your coconut oil and almond butter.

Spread this over your creamed coconut. Place the bars in your freezer for approximately 5 to 8 minutes.

4. Second Icing: Using your whisk, mix your icing together in a bowl. Drizzle your icing over the bars.

5. Store in freezer until ready to serve.

6. Serve and Enjoy!

Chocolate Drizzled Coconut Oil Fat Bombs (Serves 14)

Ingredients:

2 cups of Shredded Unsweetened Coconut

4 ounces of Raw Dark Chocolate Chips

2 tablespoons of Raw Honey

1/3 cup of Melted Coconut Oil

1/2 tablespoon of Vanilla Bean Powder (Optional)

Directions:

1. In your blender, add your shredded coconut, raw honey, coconut oil, and vanilla bean powder. Blend until your mixture is fine and crumbled.

2. Line your small-sized baking sheet or plate with wax paper. Using your tablespoon-size measuring spoon, scoop mixture and form into small-sized mounds, using your hands. Set onto your wax paper.

3. Place in your freezer for approximately 10 minutes to set.

4. Using your double boiler, melt your chocolate until smooth.

5. Use a butter knife to drizzle your coconut bombs with chocolate. Place back into your refrigerator for approximately 10 minutes.

6. Store in your refrigerator until ready to serve.

7. Serve and Enjoy!

Coconut Berry Fat Bombs

Ingredients:

1/2 cup of Mixed Frozen Berries (Cherries, Raspberries, Strawberries, Blueberries, or Pomegranates)

1 cup of Virgin Coconut Oil

14 drops of Sweet Leaf Clear Liquid Stevia

1 teaspoon of Vanilla Extract

Directions:

1. Melt your coconut oil on your stove. While your oil is melting, briefly process your frozen fruit in a food processor so it's chopped up into small-sized pieces.

2. Add your stevia and vanilla extract to your food processor.

3. Pour your melted coconut oil into your food processor and process to mix with your fruit and other ingredients. Continue to mix until all of your fruit is smoothly blended into your oil.

4. The mixture should now be a thick blended consistency. If for some reason your mixture is still frozen and not blending properly, you can remove some of the frozen bits and melt them on your stove. Once melted, return your mixture to your food processor and try again to mix everything together smoothly.

5. Scoop the finished mixture into your molds or simply drop spoonfuls on your parchment paper-lined surface such as a cutting board.

6. Put your molds or parchment paper-lined surface into your freezer to firm up the fat bombs. After approximately 30 minutes, or whenever they become solid, remove from fat bombs from the molds or parchment paper and store in a container in your freezer.

7. Serve and Enjoy!

Craving Fighter Fat Bombs (Serves 32)

Ingredients:

1 cup of Melted Organic Coconut Oil

1 cup of Almond Butter (No Added Sugar)

1 cup of Organic Cacao Powder

Directions:

1. Melt your coconut oil and whisk in your cacao and almond butter until no lumps remain. Spoon 1/2 tablespoon of your mixture into each of your 32 small paper muffin cups.

2. Refrigerate or freeze until hard.

3. Store in your refrigerator.

4. Serve and Enjoy!

Nutrition Facts:

Calories: 123

Carbs: 2.25 grams

Fat: 11.75 grams

Sugar: 0.5 grams

Cheesecake Lemon Bombs (Serves 12)

Ingredients:

4 tablespoons of Softened Unsalted Butter

1/4 cup of Melted Coconut Oil

4 ounces of Softened Cream Cheese

1 teaspoon of Lemon Juice

1 tablespoons of Finely Grated Lemon Zest

Lemon Extract (Optional)

Stevia (To Taste)

Directions:

1. Blend all of your ingredients with your hand mixer until smooth.

2. Pour into your cupcake liners, tins, or molds.

3. Freeze until firm. At least a few hours but preferably overnight.

4. Sprinkle with your lemon zest.

5. Serve and Enjoy!

Nutrition Facts:

Calories: 105

Net Carbs: .25 grams

Pumpkin Pie Fat Bombs (Serves 24)

Ingredients:

1/2 cup of Coconut Oil

1 cup of Unsweetened Long Shredded Coconut

3/4 cup of Unsweetened Pumpkin Puree

1/4 teaspoon of Himalayan Rock Salt

1 1/2 teaspoons of Ground Ginger

1 tablespoon of Ground Cinnamon

1/4 teaspoon of Alcohol-Free Pure Vanilla Extract

25 drops of Alcohol-Free Stevia Extract

Pinch of Ground Cloves

1/4 cup of Grass-Fed Collagen (Optional)

Directions:

1. Line your baking sheet with two 12-count mini muffin silicone molds. Set to the side.

2. Add your shredded coconut, stevia, coconut oil, and salt to the bowl of your food processor. Process on high for approximately 5 to 8 minutes until drippy. You may have to remove your lid a couple of times and scrape the chunkier bits from the side of your bowl.

3. Once smooth, remove 1/4 cup of your coconut mixture, leaving your remaining coconut mix in your food processor bowl. Add your remaining ingredients and process until smooth again. If you use cold pumpkin puree, the coconut will harden. Just process until smooth again.

4. The texture of your pumpkin mixture will be similar to applesauce.

5. Divide your pumpkin mixture into your muffin cups. Press down until completely flat. Top with your reserved white coconut mixture. Transfer your baking sheet to the freezer and freeze for approximately 1 hour.

6. Serve and Enjoy!

Nutrition Facts:

Calories: 219

Calories From Fat: 182

Net Carbs: 2.4 grams

Sugars: 1.9 Grams

Chocolate Frozen Whips (Serves 12)

Ingredients:

4 tablespoons of Cocoa Powder

1 cup of Heavy Whipping Cream

1/2 teaspoon of Vanilla Extract

2 1/2 tablespoons of Swerve Sweetener

1 pinch of Sea Salt

Directions:

1. Put all your ingredients into your large-sized mixing bowl and beat on high with your whip attachment until the whipped cream has firm peaks.

2. Transfer your chocolate whipped cream to a piping bag fitted with a 1M piping tip.

3. On your parchment lined baking sheet swirl the whipped cream around into large mounds like soft serve ice cream. Make around 12 or so and freeze on your baking sheet for approximately 1 hour.

4. Store in a container and place in the freezer.

5. Serve and Enjoy!

Nutrition Facts:

Calories: 70

Net Carbs: 1.5 grams

Fudge Fat Bombs (Serves 30)

Ingredients:

1/2 cup of Unsweetened Cocoa Powder

1 cup of Almond Butter

1/3 cup of Coconut Flour

1 cup of Coconut Oil (Room Temperature)

1/4 teaspoon of Powdered Stevia

1/16 teaspoon of Pink Himalayan Salt

Directions:

1. Over a medium heat in your small-sized pot, melt and combine your almond butter and coconut oil.

2. In your same pot, add your dried ingredients and stir until well-combined.

3. Allow your mixture to cool slightly and taste test to determine if additional sweetener is needed.

4. Pour mixture into your bowl and place in freezer for approximately 90 minutes or pour into silicone mold (if you choose to use a silicone mold, skip steps #5 and #6 and just allow the fat bombs to solidify in freezer, approximately 3 to 4 hours).

5. Once solidified, remove the bowl from your freezer and form into balls.

6. Place your formed balls on a flat tray or plate and return to your freezer for approximately 15 to 20 minutes.

7. Serve and Enjoy!

Nutrition Facts:

Calories: 128

Net Carbs: 1.4 grams

Ginger Fat Bombs (Serves 10)

Ingredients:

3 ounces of Softened Coconut Oil

3 ounces of Softened Coconut Butter

1 teaspoon of Granulated Sweetener

1/4 cup of Unsweetened Shredded Coconut

1 teaspoon of Ginger Powder

Directions:

1. Mix all your ingredients in a pouring jug until your sweetener is dissolved.

2. Pour mixture into your silicone molds or ice block trays and refrigerate for approximately 10 to 15 minutes.

3. Serve and Enjoy!

Nutrition Facts:

Calories: 120

Carbs: 2.2 grams

Fat: 12.8 grams

Cashew & Cacao Fat Bombs (Serves 20)

Ingredients:

1 cup of Almond Butter

1 cup of Coconut Oil

1/2 cup of Cacao Powder

1/4 cup of Coconut Flour

1 cup of Raw Cashews

Directions:

1. In your non-stick medium saucepan over a medium heat, heat your coconut oil, and almond butter until mixed evenly, stirring often.

2. Pour your oil mixture from the pan into your bowl and mix in coconut flour and cacao powder.

3. Place your bowl in your freezer for approximately 15 minutes until your mixture cools and is solid.

4. While your mixture is cooling, place your cashews in a food processor and pulse lightly for a chopped texture.

5. When your coconut mixture is solidified, take 1/2 tablespoon of your mixture from the bowl, roll into a ball, and dip in the blended cashews.

6. Place your fat bombs on a plate. Repeat until you have used all of your mixture.

7. Refrigerate the fat bombs for approximately 5 minutes.

8. Make sure to store your leftover fat bombs in the refrigerator, otherwise they will melt quickly.

9. Serve and Enjoy!

Nutrition Facts:

Calories: 217

Carbs: 6.6 grams

Fat: 20.7 grams

Pecan Pie Clusters

Ingredients:

1 cup of Chopped Pecans

3 tablespoons of Butter

2 ounces of Chopped Dark or Sugar Free Chocolate

2 tablespoons of Zen Sweet

1/4 cup of Heavy Cream

1 teaspoon of Vanilla

Directions:

1. Over a medium heat, brown your butter until golden. Stir frequently being careful not to burn.

2. Once golden, add your heavy cream and whisk together. Turn down heat to a simmer.

3. Whisking quickly, add your sweetener and vanilla, being sure to break up any lumps.

4. Continue whisking occasionally for approximately 5 minutes as your mixture begins to thicken.

5. Mixture will have consistency similar to caramel and slightly darken. Remove from the heat.

6. Mix in your chopped pecans and spoon clusters onto parchment lined tray or plate.

7. Place in freezer for approximately 5 minutes.

8. Microwave your dark chocolate for 20 to 40 seconds until melted and smooth. Drizzle over clusters.

9. Serve and Enjoy!

Nutrition Facts:

Calories: 140

Carbs: 1 gram

Peppermint Coffee Fat Bombs (Serves 12)

Ingredients:

4 tablespoons of Coconut Oil

1/4 cup of Ghee

6 squares of 100% Cacao Unsweetened Chocolate Premium Baking Bar

2 teaspoons of Peppermint Extract

36 to 48 drops of Liquid Stevia (to taste)

2 tablespoons of Heavy Whipping Cream

Directions:

1. Melt your ghee and coconut oil in your microwave safe bowl.

2. Add in six squares of 100% Cacao Unsweetened Chocolate Premium Baking Bar Chocolate and heat for 30 second intervals until melted.

3. After your oil and chocolate is melted add your peppermint extract and liquid stevia and pour your mixture into mini silicone baking cups.

4. Place chocolate cups into your freezer for at least one hour or more until frozen.

5. Optional: Place one fat bomb into a coffee cup and brew coffee over your fat bomb. Froth 2 tablespoons of heavy whipping cream and add to your coffee.

6. Serve and Enjoy!

Nutrition Facts:

Calories: 115

Net Carbs: 2 grams

Key Lime Pie Fat Bombs (Serves 30)

Ingredients:

3/4 cup of Key Lime Juice

2 cups of Raw Cashews (Boiled for 12 minutes or Soaked for 2 hours)

1/2 cup of Coconut Butter

1 cup of Melted Coconut Oil

1/4 teaspoon of Powdered Stevia

Directions:

1. Combine all of your ingredients in your food processor and blend until well combined.

2. Transfer your mixture to a medium-sized bowl and place in freezer for approximately 20 to 30 minutes to cool.

3. Remove the mixture from your freezer and form into balls.

4. Place the balls in your freezer for approximately 20 minutes to harden. Place on a cookie sheet or plate lined with parchment paper to avoid the bottoms sticking.

5. Remove from your freezer once solid. Store in an airtight container in the refrigerator or freezer.

6. Serve and Enjoy!

Nutrition Facts:

Calories: 153

Carbs: 4 grams

Maple Almond Fudge Fat Bombs (Serves 24)

Ingredients:

1/2 cup of All Natural Almond Butter

1/4 cup of Butter

2 tablespoons of Coconut Oil

1 tablespoon of Sugar-Free Zero-Carb Maple Syrup

Directions:

1. Melt your almond butter, butter, and coconut oil in the microwave for approximately 2 minutes, stirring every 30 seconds, or until smooth and fully melted together.

2. Whisk in your maple syrup and stir well to combine.

3. Pour your mixture into bite-sized paper liners set inside a mini muffin tin.

4. Refrigerate or freeze until hardened.

5. You may store these at room temperature for a soft consistency or in the freezer or fridge for a firmer consistency.

6. Serve and Enjoy!

Nutrition Facts:

Calories: 58

Carbs: 1.5 grams

Mocha Ice Bombs (Serves 12)

Ingredients:

Mocha Ice Bombs:

1 cup of Cream Cheese or Mascarpone

2 tablespoons of Cocoa Unsweetened

4 tablespoons of Powdered Sweetener

4 tablespoons of Strong Coffee (Chilled)

Chocolate Coating:

2/3 cup of Melted 90% Chocolate

1/3 cup of Melted Cocoa Butter

Directions:

1. Mocha ice bombs can be made in your food processor, or in your mixing bowl using a hand blender.

2. Add your coffee to your cream cheese, cocoa, and sweetener.

3. Pulse or blend until smooth.

4. Roll about 2 tablespoons of your mocha ice bomb mixture and place them onto a tray or plate lined with baking parchment.

5. Mix your melted chocolate and cocoa butter together.

6. Roll each mocha ice bomb in your chocolate coating and place back on your lined plate.

7. Place in your freezer for approximately 2 hours, or until set.

8. Serve and Enjoy!

Nutrition Facts:

Calories: 127

Carbs: 2.2 grams

Raspberry Almond Chocolate Fat Bombs (Serves 8)

Ingredients:

1/2 cup of Coconut Butter

1/4 cup of Almond Butter

1/4 cup of Raw Almonds

1 tablespoon of Unsweetened Cocoa Powder

1/4 cup of Walnuts

1/4 teaspoon of Stevia Powder

1/4 cup of Frozen Raspberries

Directions:

1. In your bowl, mix together your coconut butter, stevia powder, almond butter, and cocoa powder.

2. Chop your walnuts and almonds.

3. Microwave your raspberries for approximately 40 to 60 seconds.

4. Place your parchment paper over a square pan and pour your chocolate butter inside. Sprinkle the nuts over and cover with your melted raspberries.

5. Place in the freezer for approximately one hour to freeze. Take it out and break it into 8 pieces.

6. Always keep frozen. You can transfer the chocolate pieces to a container after it's frozen.

7. Serve and Enjoy!

Nutrition Facts:

Calories: 82

Carbs: 3.1 grams

Samoa Fudge Fat Bombs (Serves 10)

Ingredients:

2 1/2 tablespoons of Melted Butter

3 1/2 tablespoons of Unsweetened Cocoa Powder

3 1/2 tablespoons of Swerve Sweetener

2 1/2 tablespoons of Melted Coconut Oil

2 tablespoons of Heavy Cream or Unsweetened Coconut Milk

Caramel Coating Ingredients:

2 1/2 tablespoons of Butter

2 tablespoons of Heavy Cream

2 1/2 tablespoons of Erythritol Swerve Sweetener

1/8 teaspoon of Vanilla Extract

1/8 teaspoon of Molasses or Low-Carb Maple Syrup

To Garnish:

1 tablespoons of Unsweetened Fine Shredded Coconut

Directions:

1. In your large-sized mixing bowl combine all your fudge bomb ingredients. Mix together thoroughly. Pour or spoon your mixture into a lightly greased candy mold, ice cube tray, or cake pop pan.

2. Freeze for approximately 15 minutes or until firm.

3. In a small-sized saucepan over a medium heat melt your 2 1/2 tablespoons of butter for your caramel coating.

4. Once melted add your 2 1/2 tablespoons of sweetener, 2 tablespoons of heavy cream, and 1/8 teaspoon of molasses. Stir and heat until bubbling. Remove from the heat and stir in 1/8 teaspoon of vanilla extract. Let your caramel sauce rest for a couple minutes until it thickens.

5. Remove your fudge bombs from the freezer and place on your baking sheet lined with parchment paper or wax paper.

6. Drizzle or spoon your caramel sauce over truffle bombs and sprinkle with your shredded coconut.

7. Store in a covered container in the refrigerator or freezer.

8. Serve and Enjoy!

Nutrition Facts:

Calories: 102

Net Carbs: 1 gram

Sea Salt Chocolate Fat Bombs (Serves 10)

Ingredients:
1/2 cup of Heavy Whipping Cream

1/2 cup of Sunflower Butter

1 teaspoon of Vanilla

2 tablespoons of Cocoa Powder

1/2 cup of Coconut Oil

1 teaspoon of Cinnamon

1/3 cup of Cream Cheese

2 teaspoons of Coarse Sea Salt

3 tablespoons of Grass-Fed Butter

Directions:

1. Whip your heavy whipping cream until soft peaks form. Add your vanilla and fold in.

2. Place sunflower butter, grass-fed butter, cream cheese, coconut oil, cinnamon, and cocoa powder into the bowl of your food processor and process until smooth.

3. Gently fold your sunflower butter mixture into whipped cream until well combined.

4. Pipe mixture into silicone molds then sprinkle with coarse sea salt and freeze approximately 6 to 8 hours or overnight.

5. Serve and Enjoy!

Blueberry Cream Fat Bombs (Serves 30)

Ingredients:

4 ounces of Soft Goat Cheese

1/2 cup of Pecans

1/2 cup of Fresh Blueberries

1/2 teaspoons of Stevia

1 teaspoon of Vanilla Extract

1 cup of Almond Flour

1/4 cup of Unsweetened Shredded Coconut

Directions:

1. Process all your ingredients in a food processor until well combined.

2. Roll mixture into 30 small fat bombs.

3. Pour your coconut flakes into a small-sized bowl and lightly roll each fat bomb in your shredded coconut.

4. Serve and Enjoy!

Nutrition Facts:

Calories: 48

Net Carbs: 1 gram

Coconut Cinnamon Fat Bombs (Serves 10)

Ingredients:

1 cup of Coconut Milk (Full Fat & Canned)

1/2 teaspoon of Nutmeg

1 teaspoon of Vanilla Extract

1 teaspoon of Stevia Powder Extract

1/2 teaspoon of Cinnamon

1 cup of Coconut Butter

1 cup of Coconut Shreds

Directions:

1. Place a glass bowl over a saucepan with a few inches of water in it to create a double boiler.

2. Place all your ingredients except shredded coconut in a double boiler over a medium heat.

3. Mix your ingredients while waiting for them to melt.

4. When all your ingredients are combined remove the bowl from your heat.

5. Place your bowl in the fridge until it is hard enough to roll into balls, approximately 30 minutes.

6. Roll your contents into 1-inch balls and roll them through your coconut shreds.

7. Place your balls on a plate and refrigerate for one hour.

8. Keep refrigerated when not serving.

9. Serve and Enjoy!

Nutrition Facts:

Calories: 341

Net Carbs: 5.4 grams

Sweet Treat Chocolate Fat Bombs (Serves 4)

Ingredients:

2 ounces of Coconut Oil

1 teaspoon of Cocoa Powder

1 ounces of Cream Cheese

2 ounces of Dark Chocolate

1/2 ounces of Torani Sugar Free Vanilla Syrup

2 ounces of Almond Butter

8 drops of EZ-Sweetz

Directions:

1. Combine all of your items except the almond butter and microwave for approximately 30 seconds.

2. Stir your ingredients, if your chocolate is not fully melted, microwave again and continue to stir.

3. Pour a base layer into the mold that you're using.

4. Use a spoon and place a dollop of almond butter in the center.

5. Fill the rest of the mold to the top.

6. Freeze until the chocolate hardens. Once hard push them out of the mold.

7. Store in the refrigerator.

8. Serve and Enjoy!

Nutrition Facts:

Calories: 298

Net Carbs: 4 grams

Pudding Fat Bombs (Serves 6)

Ingredients:

1 box of Sugar-Free Jell-O Instant Pudding (Any Flavor)

3 cups of Heavy Whipping Cream

Directions:

1. Follow the instructions listed on the instant pudding box substituting the whipping cream for milk.

2. Store in the refrigerator once finished.

3. Serve and Enjoy!

Nutrition Facts:

Calories: 197

Net Carbs: 11 grams

Strawberry Shortcake Keto Fat Bombs (Serves 25)

Ingredients:

3/4 cup of Almond Flour

1/4 cup of Shredded Coconut

1/4 cup of Coconut Flour

1 teaspoon of Vanilla Extract

1/2 cup of Strawberries

1 teaspoon of Stevia

1 tablespoon of Coconut Oil

Directions:

1. Add all of your ingredients to a food processor and process until well combined.

2. Roll into 25 individual bites. If desired, roll in your shredded coconut.

3. Chill in the refrigerator for at least 1 hour.

4. Serve and Enjoy!

Nutrition Facts:

Calories: 34

Carbs: 2 grams

Fat: 2 grams

Coconut Orange Creamsicle Fat Bombs (Serves 10)

Ingredients:

1/2 cup of Coconut Oil

4 ounces of Cream Cheese

1/2 cup of Heavy Whipping Cream

10 drops of Liquid Stevia

1 teaspoon of Orange Vanilla Mio

Directions:

1. Measure out your coconut oil, heavy cream, and cream cheese.

2. Use an immersion blender to blend together all of your ingredients. If you're having a hard time blending the ingredients, you can microwave them for 30 seconds to 1 minute to soften them up.

3. Add your orange vanilla mio and liquid stevia into the mixture. Mix together with a spoon.

4. Spread your mixture into a silicone tray and freeze for approximately 2 to 3 hours.

5. Once hardened, remove from your silicone tray and store in your freezer.

6. Serve and Enjoy!

Nutrition Facts:

Calories: 178

Net Carbs: 1 gram

Chocolate Peanut Butter Fat Bombs (Serves 8)

Ingredients:

2 tablespoons of Heavy Cream

1/2 cup of Coconut Oil

6 tablespoons of Shelled Hemp Seeds

1/4 cup of Cocoa Powder

4 tablespoons of PB Fit Powder

1/4 cup of Unsweetened Shredded Coconut

1 teaspoon of Vanilla Extract

28 drops of Liquid Stevia

Directions:

1. Mix together all of your dry ingredients with the coconut oil. It will eventually turn into a paste.

2. Add vanilla, heavy cream, and liquid stevia. Mix again until everything is combined and slightly creamy.

3. Measure out unsweetened shredded coconut on to your plate.

4. Roll balls out using your hand and then roll in the unsweetened shredded coconut. Lay on to a baking tray covered with parchment paper. Set in the freezer for approximately 20 minutes.

5. Serve and Enjoy!

Nutrition Facts:

Calories: 210

Net Carbs: 1 gram

Cookie Dough Keto Fat Bombs (Serves 30)

Ingredients:

2 cups of Almond Flour

8 tablespoons of Softened Butter

1/2 teaspoon of Pure Vanilla Extract

1/3 cup of Swerve

2/3 cup of Lily's Dark Chocolate Chips

1/2 teaspoon of Kosher Salt

Directions:

1. In a large-sized bowl using a hand mixer, beat butter until light and fluffy. Add your vanilla, sugar, and salt and beat until well combined.

2. Slowly beat in your almond flour until no dry spots remain, then fold in your chocolate chips. Cover bowl with plastic wrap and place in your refrigerator to firm slightly approximately 15 to 20 minutes.

3. Using a small cookie scoop, scoop dough into small-sized balls. Store in your refrigerator if planning to eat within the week, or in the freezer for up to 1 month.

4. Serve and Enjoy!

Chocolate Walnut Fat Bombs (Serves 30)

Ingredients:

3 1/2 ounces of Dark Chocolate (85% Cocoa Solids)

1/3 cup of Small Walnut Pieces

1/4 cup of Coconut Oil

8 drops of Stevia

1 teaspoon of Cinnamon

Directions:

1. Melt your chocolate and coconut oil.

2. Crush your walnuts until you have small pieces.

3. Add your stevia, crushed walnuts, and cinnamon to your melted chocolate and coconut oil mix.

4. Pour into silicone molds or ice cube tray and freeze for approximately 5 minutes until the tops are set.

5. Remove from your freezer and press the larger walnut pieces on top.

6. Place in the refrigerator for approximately 20 minutes until your fat bombs have set.

7. Serve and Enjoy!

Nutrition Facts:

Calories: 46

Carbs: 0.7 grams

Fat: 4.8 grams

Everything Bagel and Lox Fat Bombs (Serves 36)

Ingredients:

4 ounces of Wild Caught Smoked Salmon

8 ounces of Organic Cultured Cream Cheese

2 Thinly Sliced Medium Scallions

Homemade Everything Bagel Seasoning

Directions:

1. Using a hand or stand mixer, beat cream cheese until fluffy.

2. Add your chopped smoked salmon and thinly sliced scallions.

3. Beat until well incorporated.

4. Roll into bite-sized balls then lightly coat in Everything Bagel Seasoning.

5. Chill 2 to 3 hours.

6. Serve and Enjoy!

Nutrition Facts:

Calories: 25

Carbs: 0.5 grams

Fat: 2 grams

Ice Cream Fat Bombs (Serves 5)

Ingredients:

4 Whole Pastured Eggs

4 Yolks From Pastured Eggs

2 teaspoons of Vanilla Bean Powder

1/3 cup of Melted Cacao Butter

1/3 cup of Xylitol or 15 to 20 drops of Alcohol-Free Stevia

1/3 cup of Melted Coconut Oil

1/4 cup of MCT Oil

8 to 10 Ice Cubes

Directions:

1. Add all ingredients but ice cubes into your high powered blender. Blend on high for approximately 2 minutes, until creamy.

2. While your blender is still running, remove the top portion of the lid and drop in 1 ice cube at a time, allowing your blender to run about 10 seconds between each ice cube. The goal here is to dilute the mixture just a bit and make it cold so it will run through the ice cream maker easier.

3. Once all of your ice has been added, pour your cold mixture into your ice cream maker and churn on high for approximately 20 to 30 minutes, depending on your ice cream maker. If you do not have an ice cream maker, transfer the mixture to your 9x5 loaf pan and place in your freezer. Set the timer for 30 minutes before taking out to stir. Repeat for 2 to 3 hours, until desired consistency is met.

4. Serve immediately as soft-serve or scoop into a 9x5 loaf pan and freeze for approximately 45 minutes. Store covered in the freezer for up to 1 week.

5. Enjoy!

Nutrition Facts:

Calories: 430

Net Carbs: 1.8 grams

Chocolate Chip Cookie Dough Fat Bombs (Serves 24)

Ingredients:

1 stick of Softened Unsalted Butter

8 ounces of Softened Cream Cheese

1/2 cup of Golden Monk Fruit Sweetener

1/2 cup of Crunchy Almond Butter

2 ounces of 100% Cacao Baker's Chocolate Bar

Directions:

1. In your mixing bowl, using an electric mixer, mix all of your ingredients excluding chocolate until well-combined.

2. Refrigerate your mixture for 30 minutes.

3. In your food processor, pulse your chocolate until broken into small-sized pieces.

4. Remove your mixing bowl from the refrigerator. Fold in your chocolate pieces, and form your mixture into balls or scoop and flatten into a silicone mold. (If forming fat bombs into balls, line your plate with parchment paper and set fat bombs on top of the parchment paper.)

5. Harden the fat bombs in your freezer for approximately 45 minutes.

6. Serve and Enjoy!

Nutrition Facts:

Calories: 98

Net Carbs: 1.2 grams

Pumpkin Spice Fat Bombs (Serves 24)

Ingredients:

4 ounces of Softened Cream Cheese

1/2 cup of Pecans

2 teaspoons of Pumpkin Pie Spice

1/2 cup of Pumpkin Puree

1/2 cup of Coconut Oil

1/4 cup of Golden Monk Fruit Sweetener

1/4 teaspoon of Cinnamon

Avocado Oil Cooking Spray

Directions:

1. In your small-sized pan over a medium heat, spray your avocado oil cooking spray and toast the pecans until fragrant. Remove from heat and set to the side to cool.

2. In your medium-sized pot over a medium-low heat, melt your coconut oil and cream cheese until well combined.

3. Pour your coconut oil and cream cheese mixture into a medium-sized bowl and add your pumpkin puree, pumpkin pie spice, and monk fruit sweetener. Mix together using your electric hand mixer.

4. Scoop your mixture into a silicone mold, top with your toasted pecans, and sprinkle with cinnamon.

5. Place your silicone mold in a freezer and freeze until solid, approximately 4 hours.

6. Pop your fat bombs out of the silicone mold.

7. Serve and Enjoy!

Nutrition Facts:

Calories: 78

Net Carbs: 1 gram

Pecan Pie Fat Bombs (Serves 18)

Ingredients:

1 1/2 cups of Pecans

1/4 cup of Coconut Butter

1/2 cup of Shredded Coconut

2 tablespoons of Flax Meal

2 tablespoons of Chia Seeds

2 tablespoons of Hemp Seeds

2 tablespoons of Pecan Butter

1 teaspoon of Vanilla Bean Ghee

1/2 teaspoon of Vanilla Bean Powder or Vanilla Extract

1 1/2 teaspoons of Cinnamon

1/4 teaspoon of Kosher Salt

Directions:

1. In the bowl of your food processor, combine all of your ingredients. Pulse for approximately 1 to 2 minutes, until the mixture starts to break down. It will first become powdery and will stick together, but still be crumbly.

2. Keep processing until the oils start to release a bit and the mixture sticks together easily. Be careful not to over process or you'll have nut butter.

3. Use a small-sized cookie scoop or a tablespoon scoop to divide your mixture into equal pieces. Use your hands to roll into balls and place on a plate or baking sheet and place in your refrigerator to firm up for approximately 30 minutes.

4. Store in an airtight container in your refrigerator or freezer.

5. Serve and Enjoy!

Nutrition Facts:

Calories: 120

Carbs: 3.8 grams

White Chocolate Raspberry Fat Bombs (Serves 12)

Ingredients:

1/2 cup of Freeze-Dried Raspberries

1/2 cup of Coconut Oil

1/4 cup of Swerve

2 ounces of Cacao Butter

Directions:

1. Line your 12-cup muffin pan with paper liners or use a silicone muffin pan.

2. Heat your coconut oil and cacao butter in your small-sized saucepan over a low heat until melted. Remove your pan from the heat.

3. Grind the freeze-dried raspberries in your food processor or blender.

4. Add your pulverized berries and sweetener to your saucepan. Stir until your sweetener is mostly dissolved.

5. Divide your mixture among the muffin cups. The raspberry powder will sink to the bottom. Stir your mixture as you pour it into each mold so each muffin cup has raspberry powder.

6. Chill for 1 hour or until firm. They'll keep in the refrigerator for a few weeks.

7. Serve and Enjoy!

Nutrition Facts:

Calories: 153

Net Carbs: 1.2 grams

Chocolate Coconut Almond Fat Bombs (Serves 30)

Ingredients:

1/2 cup of Melted Coconut Oil

1/4 cup of Cacao Powder or Cocoa Powder

1/2 cup of Melted Coconut Butter

1/2 teaspoon of Vanilla Extract

1 teaspoon of Almond Extract

1/4 cup of Crushed Sliced Almonds

1/4 cup of Unsweetened Finely Shredded Coconut

10 drops of Stevia (or 1/2 teaspoon of Erythritol)

1/4 cup of Cacao Nibs

Directions:

1. Mix your almond extract, coconut oil, cacao powder, coconut butter, stevia, and vanilla extract together. If using erythritol: heat in the microwave or on a stove for 1 to 2 minutes until the erythritol is dissolved.

2. Add your crushed slivered almonds, cacao nibs, and coconut flakes. With a tablespoon, fill your mini cupcake liners or an ice cube tray, putting 1 tablespoonful in each. Store in your refrigerator.

3. Serve and Enjoy!

Nutrition Facts:

Calories: 72

Carbs: 1 gram

Fat: 7 grams

Layered Peppermint Patties Fat Bombs (Serves 24)

Ingredients:

1/2 cup of Coconut Butter

2 tablespoons of Coconut Oil

1/4 cup of Unsweetened Shredded Coconut

4 ounces of 100% Dark Chocolate

1 teaspoon of Peppermint Extract

4 tablespoons of Coconut Oil

Stevia

Directions:

1. Soften your coconut butter and 2 tablespoons of coconut oil and mix together with your unsweetened shredded coconut, stevia, and peppermint extract.

2. Spoon 2 teaspoons into each of your mini muffin cups and set in the refrigerator for approximately 1 hour. Check this layer is solid before proceeding to the next step.

3. Melt 4 tablespoons of coconut oil and dark chocolate and mix together well. Spoon 1 teaspoon into each mini muffin cup so that it forms a layer. Set in your refrigerator for approximately 1 hour. Check this layer is solid before going to the next step.

4. You can repeat steps 2 and 3 for as many layers as you want.

5. Serve and Enjoy!

Nutrition Facts:

Calories: 100

Net Carbs: 2 grams

Vanilla Fat Bombs Dipped In Chocolate Fat Bombs (Serves 16)

Ingredients:

1/4 cup of 100% Dark Chocolate

1 cup of Coconut Butter

1 cup of Unsweetened Shredded Coconut

1 cup of Coconut Milk

1 tablespoon of Vanilla Extract

Stevia

Directions:

1. Melt your coconut butter and the coconut milk in a saucepan over a low heat.

2. Add in all of your ingredients except for the dark chocolate into your saucepan.

3. Mix together well. Let your mixture cool in the refrigerator for approximately 1 to 2 hours.

4. Then form small balls from your mixture (approximately 15 to 20). Place your balls into the refrigerator to solidify for 2 to 3 hours.

5. Melt your dark chocolate (in the microwave or on the stove).

6. Dip each of your balls into the chocolate, and place your dipped balls onto the parchment paper. Place back into your refrigerator.

7. Serve and Enjoy!

Nutrition Facts:

Calories: 180

Net Carbs: 3 grams

Chocolate Almond Fat Bombs (Serves 15)

Ingredients:

1 cup of Coconut Oil

1 cup of Almond Butter

1/4 cup of Coconut Flour

1/2 cup of Cacao Powder

10 to 15 Whole Almonds

Stevia

Directions:

1. Melt your almond butter and coconut oil in a saucepan. Add in your cacao powder, stevia, and coconut flour and mix together well.

2. Let your mixture cool and then form 10 to 15 small-sized balls from your mixture.

3. Stick an almond into the middle of each.

4. Refrigerate to set and store in your refrigerator.

5. Serve and Enjoy!

Nutrition Facts:

Calories: 260

Net Carbs: 3 grams

Fudge Macadamia Chocolate Fat Bombs (Serves 6)

Ingredients:

4 ounces of Chopped Macadamias

2 ounces of Cocoa Butter

2 tablespoons of Swerve

2 tablespoons of Unsweetened Cocoa Powder

1/4 cup of Heavy Cream or Coconut Oil

Directions:

1. Melt your cocoa butter in your small-sized saucepan in a bath of water. (I just use another slightly bigger saucepan, half full of water)

2. Add cocoa powder to your saucepan.

3. Add the swerve and mix well until all your ingredients are well blended and melted.

4. Add the macadamias and stir in well.

5. Add your cream, mix well and bring back to temperature.

6. Now pour in your molds or paper candy cups.

7. Allow it to cool, then put in the refrigerator to harden.

8. Keep at room temperature, with a slightly softer consistency than chocolate.

9. Serve and Enjoy!

Nutrition Facts:

Calories: 267

Carbs: 3 grams

Fat: 28 grams

Triple Layer Choconut Almond Butter Cups (Serves 12)

Ingredients:

Bottom Layer:

1/2 cup of Finely Chopped Cacao Paste

1/4 cup of Coconut Oil

1 teaspoon of Vanilla Powder

1/4 teaspoon of Ground Ceylon Cinnamon

2 to 3 drops of Pure Almond Extract

Middle Layer:

1/2 cup of All-Natural Almond Butter

1/4 cup of Coconut Oil

1/4 teaspoon of Ground Ceylon Cinnamon

Top Layer:

1/4 cup of Coconut Oil

1/2 cup of Creamy Coconut Butter

Garnish:

Whole Raw Almonds

Toasted Coconut Flakes

Directions:

1. Line your muffin pan with large parchment paper cups or silicone cups.

2. Melt 3/4 cup of coconut oil.

3. In your small-sized mixing bowl melt your cacao paste in the microwave in 20 to 30 second intervals and stir well for an equal amount of time between each melting session until there are no lumps left. Stir in 1/4 cup of the melted coconut oil, as well as your vanilla powder, cinnamon, and almond extract. Mix lightly until well combined.

4. Divide your melted chocolate equally between your 12 muffin cups and place in your refrigerator to set for approximately 5 minutes.

5. In a separate mixing bowl, add your almond butter, 1/4 cup of melted coconut oil, and ground cinnamon. Stir to combine, then pour your mixture over the set chocolate. Put your cups back into your refrigerator until that new layer has set. Should take approximately 5 to 10.

6. While your cups are in the refrigerator add 1/2 cup of creamy coconut butter to your bowl that you melted your coconut oil in (there should be 1/4 cup of oil left in it) and stir until well incorporated.

7. Gently spoon your mixture over the almond butter layer, then garnish each cup with a whole almond or a pinch of toasted coconut flakes.

8. Place in your refrigerator to finish setting, approximately 1 hour. These will keep for a few weeks if stored in the refrigerator in an airtight container.

9. Serve and Enjoy!

Nutrition Facts:

Calories: 298

Carbs: 6.5 grams

Fat: 29.5 grams

Matcha Coconut Fat Bombs (Serves 32)

Ingredients:

Main:

1/2 cup of Full Fat Coconut Milk (Refrigerated Overnight)

1 cup of Creamy Coconut Butter

1 cup of Firm Coconut Oil (Refrigerated Overnight)

1/2 teaspoon of Matcha Green Tea Powder

1/4 teaspoon of Himalayan Salt

1/4 teaspoon of Ground Ceylon Cinnamon

1 teaspoon of Pure Vanilla Extract

Coating:

1 cup of Finely Shredded Unsweetened Coconut

1 tablespoon of Matcha Green Tea Powder

Directions:

1. Add all the ingredients listed under "main" to a large-sized mixing bowl. Note that it's of utmost importance that your coconut oil be firm so send it to your refrigerator if you have to. Same goes for your coconut milk.

2. Mix on high speed with your hand mixer, until light and fluffy, then send to your refrigerator to firm up for about an hour.

3. While your mixture is firming up, combine your shredded coconut and matcha powder together in a large-sized mixing bowl. Set to the side.

4. Form the cold mixture into 32 small balls.

5. Roll your balls quickly between the palms of your hands to shape them, then drop each ball into your coconut / matcha mixture and roll them until completely coated.

6. Transfer your finished fat bombs to an airtight container and keep refrigerated for up to 2 weeks.

7. Serve and Enjoy!

Nutrition Facts:

Calories: 135

Carbs: 3 grams

Fat: 14 grams

Cardamom Orange Walnut Truffles (Serves 12)

Ingredients:
1 cup of Almond Butter

1/4 cup of Unsweetened Coconut Flakes or Shredded Coconut

1/4 cup of Coconut Oil

1/3 cup of Walnuts

2 teaspoons of Orange Zest

1/2 cup of Unsweetened Shredded Coconut

Dash of Cardamom

Stevia

1 tablespoon of Cacao Powder (Optional)

Directions:

1. Place all of your ingredients except for your 1/2 cup of shredded coconut into a blender and blend well.

2. Place in your refrigerator or freezer to solidify.

3. Form small-sized balls from your mixture.

4. Roll your balls in the remaining 1/4 cup of shredded coconut.

5. Place in your refrigerator to set.

6. Serve and Enjoy!

Nutrition Facts:

Calories: 190

Net Carbs: 3 grams

Sugar-Free Maple Nut Fudge (Serves 24)

Ingredients:

8 ounce package of Mascarpone or Cream Cheese

1 cup of Organic Butter

1/4 cup of Swerve

1 teaspoon of Maple Extract

1 teaspoon of Stevia Glycerite

Options:

1/4 teaspoon of Ground Ginger

1 cup of Pecans or Walnuts

Directions:

1. In your small-sized saucepan, melt butter over a medium-high heat (heat until it turns brown, not black).

2. Add natural sweeteners until sweeteners dissolve and the mixture bubbles just a little.

3. Using a hand mixer on a low speed, add in extract and mascarpone.

4. Mix until well combined.

5. The mixture will not emulsify until it cools a little. I placed the mixture into my blender and combined until smooth which caused it to not separate. If you use a hand mixer, it keeps separating until cooled. So after it cools a bit, whip it together.

6. Stir in the nuts and ginger if using.

7. Place a piece of parchment in an 8 x 8 square baking pan. Pour your mixture into the pan lined with parchment. Refrigerate overnight, the mixture will thicken a lot. Remove from your pan, peel away parchment and cut into 1-inch cubes. Makes 24 servings.

8. Serve and Enjoy!

Nutrition Facts:

Calories: 110

Carbs: 19 grams

Sugar-Free Mounds Bars (Serves 24)

Ingredients:

1/3 cup of Organic Extra Virgin Coconut Oil

1/3 cup of Organic Coconut Milk

1/2 cup of Confectioner's Style Swerve

1 cup of Unsweetened Organic Finely Shredded Coconut

8 ounces of Dark Chocolate (85% Cacao)

Directions:

1. In your medium-sized saucepan, combine your coconut oil, coconut milk, and the sweetener.

2. Heat over a low heat, constantly mixing until the coconut oil has melted.

3. Add your shredded coconut and mix until well mixed.

4. Pour your mixture in a 9 x 5 inch silicone loaf pan. Press your mixture tightly and evenly to the bottom of your pan.

5. Refrigerate for 3 hours or until your mixture is solid.

6. Turn your pan upside down, gently press the bottom of your pan so that the solid mixture pops out.

7. Cut your mixture into bars.

8. Chop your chocolate into small-sized pieces, equal in size.

9. Melt 3 ounces of your chopped chocolate in a water bath or in a double boiler. Don't let the chocolate get too hot, heat it gently until it is melted, stirring occasionally.

10. Remove your melted chocolate from the heat. Add 1 ounce of chopped chocolate to your melted chocolate and mix occasionally to get a smooth mixture.

11. Dip your bars in the melted chocolate, put on parchment paper or on cooling rack and let the chocolate set.

12. When your chocolate coating is completely set, melt 3 ounces of the chopped chocolate in a water bath or in a double boiler. Don't let your chocolate get too hot, heat it gently until it is melted, stirring occasionally.

13. Remove the chocolate from your heat. Add the rest of your chopped chocolate (1 ounce) to your melted chocolate and mix occasionally to get a smooth mixture.

14. Dip your bars a second time in your melted chocolate, put on parchment paper or on cooling rack and allow your chocolate to set.

15. Serve and Enjoy!

Nutrition Facts:

Calories: 110

Net Carbs: 2.1 grams

Vanilla Fat Bombs (Serves 14)

Ingredients:

1 cup of Unsalted Macadamia Nuts

1/4 cup of Virgin Coconut Oil

1/4 cup of Butter

1 Vanilla Bean or 2 teaspoon of Sugar-Free Vanilla Extract

Optional:

10 to 15 drops of Stevia Extract

2 tablespoons of Swerve

Directions:

1. Place your macadamia nuts into your blender and pulse until smooth.

2. Mix with your softened butter and coconut oil (room temperature or melted in a water bath).

3. Add swerve, stevia, and vanilla bean.

4. Pour into your mini muffin forms or an ice cube tray. You should be able to fill each one about 1 1/2 tablespoons of your mixture to get 14 servings. Place in the refrigerator for approximately 30 minutes and let it solidify.

5. When done, keep refrigerated. Coconut oil and butter get soft at room temperature.

6. Serve and Enjoy!

Nutrition Facts:

Calories: 132

Net Carbs: 0.6 grams

Mint Fudge Fat Bombs

Ingredients:

1 1/2 cups of Coconut Oil

1 1/5 cups of Nut or Seed Butter

1/2 cup of Sweetener

1/2 cup of Dried Parsley Flakes

2 tablespoons of Vanilla

1 teaspoon of Peppermint Extract

1/4 tablespoon of Salt

Melted Chocolate

Directions:

1. Melt your coconut oil in a small-sized saucepan. Add your remaining ingredients to your blender, add your coconut oil and blend until smooth.

2. Pour into an 8x8 baking pan and freeze until solid.

3. Store in your refrigerator to prevent softening.

4. Serve and Enjoy!

Keto Fat Bomb Ice Cream (Serves 5)

Ingredients:

4 Yolks from Pastured Eggs

4 Whole Pastured Eggs

1/3 cup of Melted Coconut Oil

1/3 cup of Melted Cacao Butter

1/4 cup of MCT Oil

1/3 cup of Xylitol or 15 to 20 drops of Alcohol-Free Stevia

2 teaspoons of Vanilla Bean Powder

8 to 10 Ice Cubes

Directions:

1. Add all your ingredients but the ice cubes into the jug of your high powered blender. Blend on high for approximately 2 minutes, until creamy.

2. While your blender is still running, remove the top portion of the lid and drop in 1 ice cube at a time, allowing your blender to run about 10 seconds between each ice cube. The goal here is to dilute the

mixture just a bit and make it cold so it will run through the ice cream maker easier.

3. Once all of your ice has been added, pour the cold mixture into your ice cream maker and churn on high for approximately 20 to 30 minutes, depending on your ice cream maker. If you do not have an ice cream maker, transfer the mixture to your 9x5 loaf pan and place in your freezer. Set your timer for approximately 30 minutes before taking it out to stir. Repeat for 2 to 3 hours, until desired consistency is met.

4. Serve immediately as soft-serve or scoop into a 9x5 loaf pan and freeze for approximately 45 minutes. Store covered in your freezer for up to a week.

5. Serve and Enjoy!

Peppermint Mocha Fat Bombs (Serves 16)

Ingredients:

3 tablespoons of Melted Coconut Oil

3/4 cup of Melted Coconut Butter

1/4 teaspoon of Peppermint Extract

3 tablespoons of Hemp Seeds

2 teaspoons of Instant Coffee Powder

2 tablespoons of Organic Cocoa Powder

5 to 8 drops of Liquid Stevia

Directions:

1. Mix together your melted coconut butter, 1 tablespoon of coconut oil, hemp seeds, and peppermint extract.

2. Pour into molds about 3/4 of the way.

3. Refrigerate until firm.

4. Stir together 2 tablespoons of melted coconut oil, cocoa powder, instant coffee, and stevia.

5. Drizzle on top of your fat bombs.

6. Refrigerate again until completely hardened.

7. Pop out of your molds and transfer to an airtight container.

8. Store in your refrigerator or freezer.

9. Serve and Enjoy!

Nutrition Facts:

Calories: 121

Carbs: 4 grams

Blackberry Coconut Fat Bombs (Serves 16)

Ingredients:

1 cup of Coconut Butter

1/2 cup of Fresh or Frozen Blackberries

1 cup of Coconut Oil

1/4 teaspoon of Vanilla Powder or 1/2 teaspoon of Vanilla Extract

1/2 teaspoon of Sweet Leaf Stevia Drops

1 tablespoon of Lemon Juice

Directions:

1. Place your coconut butter, coconut oil, and blackberries (if frozen) in a pot and heat over a medium heat until well combined.

2. In your food processor or small blender, add your coconut oil mix and remaining ingredients. Process until smooth. Separation may occur if coconut oil mixture is too hot. If using fresh berries, there is no need to cook them with the coconut oil and butter.

3. Spread out into a small-sized pan lined with parchment paper (I used a 6x6-inch container)

4. Refrigerate for one hour or until your mix has hardened.

5. Remove from your container and cut into squares.

6. Store covered in the refrigerator.

7. Serve and Enjoy!

Nutrition Facts:

Calories: 170

Carbs: 3 grams

Fat: 19 grams

White Chocolate Coconut Fudge (Serves 24)

Ingredients:

4 ounces of Cacao Butter

1/2 cup of Coconut Oil

15-ounce can of Coconut Milk

1 cup of Coconut Butter

1 teaspoon of Vanilla Extract

1/2 cup of Vanilla Protein Powder

1 teaspoon of Coconut Liquid Stevia

Pinch of Salt

Optional:

Unsweetened Coconut Flake

Directions:

1. Melt your cacao butter in your saucepan over a low heat.

2. Stir in your coconut milk, coconut oil, and coconut butter.

3. Continue to stir until completely smooth, no lumps.

4. Turn off your heat and whisk in protein powder, vanilla extract, stevia, and salt.

5. Pour your mixture into a parchment lined 8x8 pan.

6. Sprinkle with coconut flakes if desired.

7. Refrigerate for 4 hours or overnight.

8. Does not need to be kept refrigerated for storage.

9. Serve and Enjoy!

Nutrition Facts:

Calories: 175

Net Carbs: 1.2 grams

Daily Greens Fat Bomb Truffles (Serves 14)

Ingredients:

1 1/2 cups of Unsweetened Medium-Shredded Coconut

1/2 cup of Extra-Virgin Coconut Oil (At Room Temperature)

2 tablespoons of Greens+ O Powder (Vanilla Flavor)

For Cacao Truffles add:

1/4 cup of Cacao Powder

Optional Toppings:

Chia seeds

Hemp hearts

Unsweetened Medium-Shredded Coconut

Directions:

1. Line your small-sized baking sheet with parchment paper and set to the side. If you're going to add toppings to your truffles, place a couple of tablespoons of topping ingredients in separate small-sized bowls and set to the side.

2. Add your coconut and greens powder to your bowl of your stand mixer or food processor with dough blade, or a large-sized bowl and use a handheld mixer. Mix until your coconut is covered in greens, then add your coconut oil.

3. Mix until everything is well combined. The mixture should hold together.

4. Scoop dough, about 1 tablespoon at a time, into the palm of your hand. Roll lightly and place on your prepared baking sheet. Repeat with your remaining dough. Mixture should make 14 truffles.

5. Once completed, transfer your baking sheet to the refrigerator to cool for approximately 15 minutes.

6. Store in an air-tight container in your refrigerator for 5 days, or freezer for 2 months.

7. Serve and Enjoy!

Nutrition Facts:

Calories: 152

Net Carbs: 1.7 grams

White Chocolate Butter Pecan Fat Bombs (Serves 4)

Ingredients:

2 tablespoons of Coconut Oil

2 ounces of Cocoa Butter

2 tablespoons of Butter

2 tablespoons of Powdered Erythritol

1/2 cup of Chopped Pecans

1/4 teaspoon of Vanilla Extract

Pinch of Salt

Pinch of Stevia

Directions:

1. Melt your coconut oil, cocoa butter, and butter together in a small-sized pan until melted. Then turn your heat off.

2. Stir in 2 tablespoons of powdered erythritol into your butter mixture until well combined.

3. Add a pinch of salt to bring out the sweetness.

4. Add in a pinch of Stevia.

5. Add in your vanilla extract.

6. Into silicone cupcake molds or candy molds, add a few chopped pecans. I added about 3-4 pecans total to each mold, but this can be altered. If you don't have pecans, walnuts and hazelnuts work well.

7. Pour your white chocolate mix evenly into the molds over your nuts and place in the freezer immediately.

8. Freeze for about 30 minutes. You want them to be nice and cool when eating as they melt easily.

9. Serve and Enjoy!

Nutrition Facts:

Calories: 287

Carbs: 0.5 grams

Fat: 30 grams

Strawberry-Filled Coconut Fat Bombs (Serves 15)

Ingredients:

1/3 cup of Coconut Butter

1/2 tablespoon of Cocoa Powder

1/3 cup of Coconut Oil + 1 tablespoon

1 tablespoons of Unsweetened Shredded Coconut

1/3 cup of Diced Fresh Strawberries

8 to 10 drops of Liquid Stevia

Directions:

1. In your bain-marie, add the coconut butter, 1/3 cup of coconut oil, cocoa powder, and a few drops of liquid stevia. Heat until fully melted.

2. Meanwhile, in your small-sized frying pan, add your fresh strawberries and a few spoonfuls of water. Cook over a medium heat until soft. Mash with a fork. Add the berries to a blender with 1 tablespoon of melted coconut oil and a few more drops of liquid stevia. Blend until smooth.

3. Fill your molds with the melted coconut mixture. Add about 1 teaspoon of the strawberry mixture into each mold. Sprinkle with a few shreds of unsweetened coconut.

4. Place in your refrigerator until fully hardened; at least a couple of hours or overnight. Pop out of the molds and store in an air-tight container in the refrigerator.

5. Serve and Enjoy!

Nutrition Facts:

Calories: 106

Net Carbs: 1 gram

No-Bake Grasshopper Bars

Ingredients:

Mint Layer:

2 Hass Avocados

3/4 cup of Melted Coconut Oil

1/2 cup of Sweetener

4 cups of Organic Shredded Unsweetened Coconut

6 scoops of Stevia

3/8 teaspoon of Organic Peppermint Extract

3/4 teaspoon of Vanilla

1/4 teaspoon of Salt

Chocolate Layer:

1/2 cup of Coconut Oil

1/2 cup of Cocoa Powder

1/8 teaspoon of Salt

1/2 teaspoon of Vanilla

1/4 cup of Xylitol (blended preferred for smoothness)

Directions:

Mint Layer:

1. Lightly grease your 8x8 pan.

2. Place all your ingredients in high powered blender or a food processor. Process until blended. If you prefer the texture of coconut in the finished result, do not process completely.

3. Spread your mixture into prepared pan and place in freezer.

Chocolate Layer:

1. In a small-sized saucepan, melt your coconut oil and sweetener over a low heat.

2. Remove from your heat, add in the remaining ingredients, and stir to combine.

3. Pour over your chilled bottom layer. Return to your freezer until the chocolate layer is solid.

4. Cut into bars

5. Store covered in the refrigerator or freezer

6. Serve and Enjoy!

No Bake N'oatmeal Fudge Bars (Serves 16)

Ingredients:

N'oatmeal Crust & Topping:

1 cup of Coconut Oil

2 cups of Manitoba Harvest Hemp Hearts

1/4 cup of Birch-Sourced Xylitol

1/3 cup of Coconut Flour

1/2 cup of Unsweetened Fancy Shredded Coconut

1/2 teaspoon of Vanilla Extract

Dairy-free Fudge:

1/2 cup of Full-Fat Coconut Milk

10 ounces of Unsweetened Chocolate

10 drops of Alcohol-Free Stevia

Directions:

1. Line your 9x9 baking sheet with parchment paper draping over all sides for easy lifting.

2. Melt your coconut oil and xylitol in a large-sized saucepan over a medium heat. Whisk until xylitol granules have dissolved, about 2 minutes.

3. Add Manitoba Harvest Hemp Hearts, shredded coconut, coconut flour, and vanilla extract. Remove from the heat and combine with a spoon until your ingredients are well blended. Press half of your mixture into the bottom of the prepared pan. Reserve the other half for topping, set to the side.

4. Transfer the base to your refrigerator while you continue with the fudge layer.

5. Meanwhile, melt your chocolate and coconut milk in a small-sized heavy saucepan over a low heat, frequently stirring until smooth. Stir in your stevia and set to the side.

6. Take the base out of your fridge. Spoon the chocolate mixture over the crust in your pan, and spread evenly with a knife or the back of a spoon. If the bottom layer hasn't totally set, a couple of hemp hearts will lift up and mix in with the chocolate, so take your time.

7. Crumble the remaining hemp mixture over your chocolate layer, pressing in gently. Cover, and refrigerate 2 to 3 hours or overnight. Cut into 16 bars and enjoy!

8. Store in the refrigerator.

9. Serve and Enjoy!

Cinnamon Coffee Cake Collagen Fat Bombs (Serves 12)

Ingredients:

1/4 cup of Almond Butter

1/2 cup of Coconut Oil

1 tablespoon of Instant Coffee

1 packet of Vanilla Collagen

1 teaspoon of Cinnamon

Directions:

1. In your small-sized saucepan heat coconut oil and almond butter on low until melted.

2. You can also microwave the coconut oil for about 30 seconds until melted.

3. Stir together all your ingredients.

4. Pour into an 8x8 pan, mini muffin tins, or silicone/plastic candy molds. Freeze until firm.

5. Serve and Enjoy!

Blackberry Mascarpone Fat Bombs (Serves 9)

Ingredients:

1/2 cup of Blackberries (No Sugar Added)

1 cup of Coconut Oil

2 tablespoons of Mascarpone Cheese

1 cup of Coconut Butter

1/2 teaspoon of Lemon Juice

1/4 teaspoon of Vanilla Extract

1/2 teaspoon of Liquid Stevia

Directions:

1. Start by thawing blackberries in a small-sized bowl.

2. Once your blackberries are thawed place your mascarpone cheese, coconut oil, coconut butter, vanilla extract, lemon juice, and liquid stevia in a mixing bowl and mix on low until everything is combined well. The smoother the better.

3. Spoon into silicone cupcake liners.

4. Freeze for 30 minutes and keep refrigerated.

5. Serve and Enjoy!

Nutrition Facts:

Calories: 437

Net Carbs: 4 grams

Conclusion

Thanks for reading my book. I hope this keto fat bombs recipe book has provided you with a nice variety of tasty treats to aid you in your ketogenic diet.

Good luck. I wish you nothing but the best!

www.ingramcontent.com/pod-product-compliance
Lightning Source LLC
Chambersburg PA
CBHW071440070526
44578CB00001B/163